MW01132613

Other books by Simon Leys

*The Life and Work of Su Renshan, Rebel,
Painter and Madman* (Prix Stanislas-Julien,
Institut de France)

*The Chairman's New Clothes: Mao and the
Cultural Revolution*

Chinese Shadows

Broken Images

The Burning Forest

The Analects of Confucius
(translation and commentary)

The Angel and the Octopus

The Wreck of the Batavia & Prosper

The Death of Napoleon

Illustrations: *The Two Acrobats*
(text by Jeanne Ryckmans)

Other People's Thoughts

Idiosyncratically
compiled by
SIMON LEYS
for the amusement
of idle readers

Published by Black Inc.,
an imprint of Schwartz Publishing Pty Ltd
Level 5, 289 Flinders Lane
Melbourne Victoria 3000 Australia
email: enquiries@blackincbooks.com
http://www.blackincbooks.com

The National Library of Australia
Cataloguing-in-Publication entry:

       Other people's thoughts.

       1st Australian ed.
       Includes index.
       ISBN 9781863954150 (pbk.).

       1. Quotations, English. I. Leys, Simon, 1935- .
       II. Title.

       082

Book design: Thomas Deverall
Printed in Australia by Griffin Press

Front cover image: *Roll of Card and Books*, 1992 (oil on
canvas) by Rohner, Georges (1913-2000) ©Private
Collection/ Giraudon/ The Bridgeman Art Library

for Hanfang

FOREWORD

'Most people are other people,' Oscar Wilde remarked, 'their thoughts are someone else's opinions, their life a mimicry, their passions a quotation … One realises one's soul only by getting rid of culture.'

And, indeed, many commonplace books remind me of a dull gentleman I knew: he collected jokes in a little notebook and, before attending social functions, he used to rehearse half-a-dozen of these in order to impress his acquaintances with his wit.

Yet all commonplace books need not be inspired by a pathetic desire to show off the sort of borrowed cultural varnish which rightly earned Wilde's scorn; they can also reflect a reality well described by Alexandre Vialatte: 'the most valuable contribution which great artists are offering is to give us not their truth, but *ours*.'

A commonplace book that would collect literary quotations on the sole basis of their eloquence, profundity, wit or beauty would be both endless and incoherent.

It can draw its inner unity only from the compiler himself, whose mind and character it should somehow mirror. By adopting such an idiosyncratic perspective, the compiler does not indulge in narcissism (see below, under entry 'I', the quote from Thoreau) – he merely follows a principle of organisation and economy.

S. L.

NOTE:

The quotations are reproduced in the language in which I found them – which is not necessarily their original language (for instance, I read Russian and German authors only in French or English translations).

All foreign-language quotations are followed by their English translations.

The headings are arranged in alphabetical order. Within each heading the different entries do not follow a systematic chronological order: they have been mixed somewhat freely, to produce variety, contrasts or parallelisms.

The authors are identified sometimes by their given names and surnames (Henry James, William James), sometimes by their surnames only (Shakespeare, Montaigne). I followed no particular rule, only ear and instinct. However, more complete information can be found in the Index of Authors at the end.

Needless to say, this is not a 'scholarly' book (on the subject of scholarship and erudition, consult under the heading SCHOLAR, the views of Prince de Ligne, Lichtenberg, Claudel and Hugo; see also, under CRITI-CISM, Auden's second quote).

ADVENTURE

~ Adventure is a product of incompetence.

—AMUNDSEN

AMBITION

L' ambition dont on n'a pas les talents est un crime.
~ An ambition without matching talent is a crime.

—CHATEAUBRIAND

Tout le mal qui est fair sur la Terre est fait par les con-vaincus et les ambitieux. Le sceptique sans ambitions est le seul être innocent sur la Terre.
~ All evil on earth is the work of people driven by con-viction and by ambition. A sceptic without ambition is the only innocent creature in this world.

—MONTHERLANT

~ The penetrating power of his mind acting like a cor-rosive fluid had destroyed his ambition.

—CONRAD

ART

Une œuvre d'art qui ne nous rend pas muets est de peu de valeur: elle est commensurable en paroles. Il en résulte que celui qui écrit sur les arts ne peut se flatter que de restituer ou de préparer ce silence de stupeur charmée: l'amour sans phrases.

~ A work of art that does not make us silent is of little value: it can find its equivalent in words. As a result, he who writes on the arts can only aim at restoring or preparing this silence of enchanted wonderment: love without phrases.

—PAUL VALÉRY

~ Life is a shit-storm in which art is our only umbrella.

—MARIO VARGAS LLOSA

~ We have art so that we do not die of the truth.

—NIETZSCHE

~ Sometimes I wonder how all those who do not write, compose or paint can manage to escape the madness, the melancholia, the panic fear which is inherent in the human situation.

—GRAHAM GREENE

~ I feel exactly as you do about our 'art', but it comes over me in a kind of rage every now and then – and then, if I don't write to empty my mind, I go mad. As to that regular, uninterrupted love of writing which you describe, I do not understand it. I feel it as a torture,

2

which I must get rid of, but never as a pleasure. On the contrary, I think composition is a great pain.

—BYRON

~ You want to know how to paint a perfect painting? It is easy. Make yourself perfect, and then just paint naturally.

—ROBERT PIRSIG

La satisfaction de l'homme qui a travaillé et convenablement employé sa journée est immense. Quand je suis dans cet état, je jouis délicieusement ensuite du repos et des moindres délassements. Je peux même, sans le moindre regret, me trouver dans la société des gens les plus ennuyeux. Le souvenir de la tâche que j'ai accomplie me revient et me préserve de l'ennui et de la tristesse.

~ The satisfaction of an artist who has employed his day well, working on a painting, is immense. When I am in that state, my enjoyment of rest or of the slightest recreation is exquisite. I can even bear without irritation the company of the dullest people. The memory of the accomplished task is still lingering in me and wards off boredom and melancholy.

—DELACROIX

ATTENTION

Comme l'on serait savant si l'on connaissait bien seulement cinq à six livres.
~ How learned we would be if we knew only five or six books well.

— FLAUBERT

L'attention absolument sans mélange est prière. Toutes les fois qu'on fait vraiment attention on détruit du mal en soi.
~ Absolutely unmixed attention is prayer. Whenever we truly pay attention, we destroy some evil in ourselves.*

— SIMONE WEIL

BALM

~ Extract your balm from your poison.

— NIETZSCHE

BAMBOO

寧可食無肉。不可居無竹。無肉令人
瘦。無竹令人俗。人瘦尚可肥。人俗
不可醫。

蘇軾

---

* See also SOLITUDE, Simone Weil's quotation.

~ Rather eat food without meat, than live in a place without bamboo. Without meat, you may become thin; but without bamboo, you will become vulgar. A thin man can still get fat; a vulgar man cannot be cured.

—Su Dongpo

BASIC NEEDS

Il me faut un ami sûr, une femme aimable, une vache et un petit bateau.
~ I need a reliable friend, a lovely woman, a cow and a little boat.

—Jean-Jacques Rousseau

BEAUTY

Toute personne est moindre que ce qu'elle a fait de plus beau.
~ Every individual is inferior to his most beautiful work.

—Paul Valéry

Je montrais à Braque un faux Braque, faux mais très bien imité, jusqu'à la signature. Comme il faisait la grimace: 'Enfin, ce sont bien là vos couleurs: ce bleu ne trompe pas, ni ce violet.' 'Ce sont bien mes couleurs.'

'C'est votre composition: ce sont bien vos traits; c'est votre atmosphère.' 'Pas de doute.' 'Vous auriez pu le peindre.' 'Croyez-vous que je ne sois pas capable de faire de faux Braque?' 'Qu'est-ce que vous lui reprochez, enfin?' 'C'est qu'il serait plutôt le contraire d'un Braque.' 'Comment l'entendez-vous?' 'Je vais vous le dire: il est beau.'

~ I was showing Braque a fake Braque – fake, yet exceedingly well imitated, down to the signature. As he winced, I said, 'Come on, these are exactly your colours: this blue, this purple are unmistakeable.' – 'They are my colours all right.' – 'And it is your composition, your style, your atmosphere.' – 'No doubt.' – 'You could have painted it yourself!' – 'Don't you think I'd be able to paint a fake Braque?' – 'Then, what fault can you find with this one?' – 'The fact that it is the exact opposite of a genuine Braque.' – 'What do you mean?' – 'I'll tell you: this thing is *beautiful.*'

—J. PAULHAN

~ Chen Hongshou (17th century) was repeatedly copying a painting by Zhou Fang (8th century). People asked him: 'Why do it again? Your copies are already much better than the original!' 'This is precisely why they are inferior. It is all too easy to see the beauty of my copies, but that is their weak point. Zhou Fang's art is supreme: where he appears clumsy, he cannot be equalled.'

—LIFE OF CHEN HONGSHOU*

BEST-SELLERS

Tout le monde ne tend à lire que ce que tout le monde aurait pu écrire.
~ Everyone tends to read what everyone could have written.

—PAUL VALÉRY

BIOGRAPHY

On se demande comment la perspective d'avoir un biographe n'a jamais découragé personne d'avoir une vie.
~ It's a wonder the prospect of having a biographer never discouraged anyone from having a life.

—CIORAN

~ Geniuses have the shortest biographies because their inner lives are led out of sight and earshot; and in the end, their cousins can tell you nothing about them.

—EMERSON

---

* See also CLUMSINESS.

L' essentiel de la biographie d'un écrivain consiste dans la liste des livres qu'il a lus.

~ The essential part of a writer's biography consists of a list of all the books he read.

—VALERY LARBAUD

BOOKS

~ Occasionally I come across a book which I feel has been written especially for me, and for me only. Like a jealous lover, I don't want anybody else to hear of it. To have a million such readers, unaware of each other's existence, to be read with passion and never talked about, is the daydream, surely, of every author.

—W. H. AUDEN

~ A book is a mirror; if an ape looks into it, an apostle is hardly likely to look out.

—LICHTENBERG

~ Buying books would be a good thing if one could also buy the time to read them in; but, as a rule, the purchase of books is mistaken for the appropriation of their contents.

—SCHOPENHAUER

~ Books are for one thing only: inspiration.

—EMERSON

CABINET MINISTER

人家養子望聰明
我被聰明誤一生
唯願我兒愚且魯
無災無難到公卿

蘇軾

'On the birth of my son'
Families, when a child is born
Want it to be intelligent.
I, through intelligence,
Having wrecked my whole life,
Only hope the baby will prove
Ignorant and stupid,
Then he will crown a tranquil life
By becoming a cabinet minister.

—Su Dongpo *(translated by Arthur Waley, 1918)*

CERTAINTY

No siempre lo peor es cíerto.
~ The worst is not always certain.

—Caldeɾ n

~ It's certainty, not doubt, that causes madness.

—Nietzsche

9

CHAIR

~ I had three chairs in my house; one for solitude, two for friendship, three for society.

—THOREAU

CHANCE

Le hasard est le dieu des imbéciles.
~ Chance is the god of morons.

—BERNANOS

CHURCH

~ The Church is the only thing that can save a man from the degrading servitude of being a child of one's time.

—CHESTERTON

Une société à prétention divine comme l'Église est peut-être plus dangereuse par l'ersatz de bien qu'elle contient que par le mal qui la souille.
~ In an institution which considers itself divine such as the Church, the imitation good it contains is perhaps more dangerous than the evil which sullies it.

—SIMONE WEIL

On ne réforme l'Église qu'en souffrant pour elle; on ne réforme l'Église visible qu'en souffrant pour l'Église invisible […] L'Église n'a pas besoin de réformateurs, mais de saints.

~ The only way to reform the Church is by suffering for her. One reforms the visible Church only by suffering for the invisible Church […] The Church does not need reformers, she needs saints.

—Bernanos

CIVILISATION

Les peuples les plus civilisés sont aussi voisins de la barbarie que le fer le plus poli l'est de la rouille. Les peuples comme les métaux n'ont de brillant que les surfaces.

~ The most civilised nations are as close to barbarity as the most polished iron is close to rust. Nations, like metals, shine only on the surface.

—Rivarol

CLOTHES

~ Beware of all enterprises that require new clothes.

—Thoreau

CLUMSINESS

拙笨

~ What I fear most of all is that my painting may look skilful.

—Gong Xian

Ai-je tort, je crains bien de n'aimer guère que les romans pour une part avortés, où l'auteur ne craint ni d'être insistant, ni d'être naïf … [Tandis que] Aurélien [d'Aragon] m'a paru détestable. Détestable et grisâtre, comme la plupart des ouvrages où un auteur 'doué' met à la fois toutes ses qualités.

~ Perhaps it's wrong of me, but I am afraid I only like novels that are partly botched, where the author is not afraid to be insistent or naïve […] Whereas [Aragon's] *Aurélien* seems to me utterly unpleasant – unpleasant and dull, like most of these works in which a 'gifted' author displays all his qualities together.

—J. PAULHAN

COGLIONI

Ridiamo insieme di questi coglioni che possiedono l'orbe terracqueo.

~ Let us laugh together at these *coglioni* who own the world.

—LEOPARDI

Qui pardonne est un chrétien, qui oublie est un coglione.

~ He who forgives is a Christian; he who forgets is a *coglione*.

—CORSICAN PROVERB

COMIC RABBITS

~ He found a formula for drawing comic rabbits.
This formula for drawing comic rabbits paid;
So, in the end, he could not change the tragic habits
This formula for drawing comic rabbits made.

—ROBERT GRAVES

COMMUNICATION

~ We are in great haste to construct a magnetic telegraph from Maine to Texas; but Maine and Texas, it may be, have nothing important to communicate.

—THOREAU

~ One inconvenience I sometimes experienced in so small a house, the difficulty of getting to a sufficient distance from my guest when we begin to utter the big thoughts in big words. You want room for your thoughts to get into sailing trim and run a course or two before they make their port […] I have found it a singular luxury to talk across a pond to a companion on the opposite side.

—THOREAU

CONSERVATIVE MANIFESTO

~ A conservative has positive work to do. Civilisation

has no force of its own beyond what is given it from within. It is under constant assault and it takes most of the energies of civilised man to keep going at all. There are criminal ideas and a criminal class in every nation and the first action of every revolution, figuratively and literally, is to open the prisons. Barbarism is never finally defeated; given propitious circumstances, men and women who seem quite orderly will commit every conceivable atrocity. The danger does not come merely from habitual hooligans; we are all potential recruits for anarchy. Unremitting effort is needed to keep men living together at peace; there is only a margin of energy left over for experiment however beneficent. Once the prisons of the mind have been opened, the orgy is on. There is no more agreeable position than that of dissident from a stable society [...] The more elaborate the society, the more vulnerable it is to attack, and the more complete its collapse in case of defeat.

—EVELYN WAUGH

CONTRACT

~ The basis of all civilised life is the observance of contracts.

—CICERO

COST

~ The cost of a thing is the amount of what I will call life which is required to be exchanged for it, immediately or in the long run.

—THOREAU

COUPLES

~ Human love, human trust are always perilous because they break down. The greater the love, the greater the trust, and the greater the peril, the greater the disaster. Because to place absolute trust in another human being is in itself a disaster, both ways, since each human being is a ship that must sail its own course, even if it goes in company with another ship. Two ships may sail together to the world's end. But lock them together in mid ocean and try to steer both with one rudder, and they will smash one another to bits. So it is when one individual seeks absolutely to love, or trust, another. Absolute lovers always smash one another, absolute trusters the same. Since man has been trying absolutely to love women, and women to love man, the human species has almost wrecked itself.

—D. H. LAWRENCE

COURAGE

~ Cowards die many times before their deaths; the valiant never taste of death but once.

—SHAKESPEARE

C'est quelquefois vaillance que vivre.
~ Merely to live is sometimes an act of courage.

—MONTAIGNE

~ The ordinariness of human lives can never be a measure of the effort it takes to keep them going.

—BALZAC*

~ Courage means not scaring others.

—PHILIP LARKIN

~ It is unworthy of a great soul to spread around himself the trouble he experiences.

—NIETZSCHE

Un couvreur prend plus de risques qu'un intellectuel.
~ A roofer takes more risks than an intellectual.

—SARTRE

---

* I found this quote on the back cover of a beautiful novel by Penelope Fitzgerald, *The Bookshop*. I could not locate its original French version.

~ I cannot conceive of any writing that would require more courage than entering a bath of cold water.

—C. S. Lewis

~ All men would be cowards if only they had the courage.

—Second Earl of Rochester

CRITICISM

Le plus grand malheur d'un homme de lettres n'est peut-être pas d'être l'objet de la jalousie de ses confrères, la victime de la cabale, le mépris des puissants de ce monde; c'est d'être jugé par des sots.

~ The greatest misfortune for a writer is perhaps not to be the target of his colleagues' jealousy, the victim of intrigue, or to be despised by the powerful; it is to be judged by fools.

—Voltaire

En vain les trompettes de la renommée ont proclamé telle prose ou tels vers: il y a toujours dans la Capitale trente ou quarante têtes incorruptibles qui se taisent. Le silence des gens de goût sert de conscience aux mauvais écrivains, et les tourmente le reste de leur vie.

~ The trumpets of fame have saluted in vain this essay or that poem: there are always in Paris thirty or forty incorruptible judges who remain silent. The silence of men of taste acts as the conscience of bad writers and torments them for the rest of their lives.

—RIVAROL

Je refuse de savoir ce que peut penser des hommes de talent un homme qui n'en a pas.
~ I reject the idea that men who have talent may be judged by a man who has none.

—JULES RENARD

Personne n'est exempt de dire des fadaises, le malheur est de les dire curieusement.
~ Anyone may say something silly; what is unfortunate is to do so earnestly.

—MONTAIGNE

~ I should like to like Schumann's music better than I do; I dare say I could make myself like it better if I tried; but I do not like having to try to make myself like things. I like things that make me like them at once, and no trying at all.

—SAMUEL BUTLER

~ When I am told what is artistic and inartistic, of realism, commitment and all that, I am baffled. I divide all works into two kinds: those I like and those I don't like. I have no other yardstick, and if you ask me why I like Shakespeare and don't like Zlatovratsky, I shall have no answer.

—CHEKHOV

~ The function of criticism, if it has a legitimate function at all, can only be one function – that of dealing with the subconscious part of the author's mind, which only the critic can express, and not with the conscious part of the author's mind, which the author himself can express. Either criticism is no good at all (a very defensible position) or else criticism means saying about an author the very things that would have made him jump out of his boots.

—CHESTERTON

~ Never trust the artist. Trust the tale. The proper function of a critic is to save the tale from the artist who created it.

—D. H. LAWRENCE

~ The only obligation to which, in advance, we may hold a novel without incurring the accusation of being arbitrary, is that it be interesting. That general responsibility rests upon it, but it is the only one I can think of. The ways in which it is at liberty to accomplish this result […] strike me as innumerable, and such as can only suffer from being marked out or fenced in by prescription.

—HENRY JAMES

~ If you do not say a thing in an irritating way, you may as well not say it at all.

—BERNARD SHAW

~ I think unless one hears a little squeal of pain after one's done some writing, one has not really done much.

—V. S. NAIPAUL

~ There can be literature without criticism, but no criticism without literature.

—M. REICH-RANICKI

~ The only sensible procedure for a critic is to keep silent about works which he believes to be bad [...] Attacking bad books is not only a waste of time but also bad for the character [...] One cannot review a bad book without showing off.

—W. H. AUDEN

On est stupéfait de la quantité de critiques que peut contenir un imbécile.
~ It's dumbfounding how much criticism can fit into one fool's head.

—VICTOR HUGO

~ In general, when reading a scholarly critic, one profits more from the quotations than from the comments.

—W. H. AUDEN

DEATH*

~ Sleep after toyle, port after stormie seas
Ease after war, death after life does greatly please.

—SPENSER

~ … all life death does end and each day dies with sleep.

—G. MANLEY HOPKINS

Je veux qu'on agisse et qu'on allonge les offices de la vie tant qu'on peut, et que la mort me trouve plantant mes choux, mais nonchalant d'elle, et encore plus de mon jardin imparfait.

~ I want us to be doing things, prolonging life's duties as much as we can. May death find me as I am working in my cabbage patch, indifferent to its coming, and even more indifferent to the imperfection of my garden.

—MONTAIGNE

À parler humainement, la mort a un bel endroit, qui est de mettre fin à la vieillesse. La mort qui prévient la caducité arrive plus à propos que celle qui la termine.

---

* See also ZHUANG ZI.

~ From a humane point of view, death has a good side, which is to put an end to old age. A death which prevents senility is more welcome than a death which concludes it.

—LA BRUYÈRE

Tous meurent. Nul ne sait mourir.

Mourir est l'ouvrage pour lequel il n'est ni apprentissage, ni expérience.

Les vivants connaissent 'l'avant' de la mort, ses préliminaires, l'agonie.

Les croyants, par la foi, envisagent 'l'après'.

Mais entre l'avant et l'après est la minute sans lumière, éternellement secrète.

Là est l'horreur inconnue.

~ All die. None knows how to die.

Death is the one undertaking for which there is neither apprenticeship nor experience.

The living know what comes before death – its preliminaries, the agony.

The believers, through faith, contemplate what will come afterwards.

But in between 'before' and 'after', there is the minute without light, forever secret.

There lies the unknown horror.

—MARIE NOËL

DECENT PEOPLE

C'est le malheur des gens honnêtes qu'ils sont des lâches.

~ The misfortune of decent people is that they are cowards.

—Voltaire

~ The only thing necessary for the triumph of evil is for good men to do nothing.

—Edmund Burke

Je ne doute pas que les honnêtes gens soient avec moi, mais j'aime qu'ils me le disent.

~ I have no doubt that all decent people are on my side, but I would like them to tell me so.

—Abbé Mugnier

DEMOCRACY

~ The demand for equality has two sources; one of them is among the noblest, the other is the basest, of human emotions. The noble source is the desire for fair play. But the other source is the hatred of superiority […] Equality (outside mathematics) is a purely social conception. It applies to man as a political and economic animal. It has no place in the world of the mind. Beauty is not democratic, virtue is not democratic, truth is not democratic. Political democracy is doomed if it tries to extend its demand for equality into these higher spheres. Ethical, intellectual, or aesthetic democracy is death. A truly democratic education – one which will preserve democracy – must be, in its own field, ruthlessly aristocratic, shamelessly 'high-brow' […] Democracy demands that little men should not take big ones too seriously; it dies when it is full of little men who think they are big themselves.

—C. S. Lewis*

Un ancien exemple de décision démocratique: la demande populaire de libérer Barabbas, et de crucifier Jésus.
~ An early example of democratic decision-making: the popular demand to free Barabbas and to crucify Jesus.

—Simone Weil

DESPAIR

Le désespoir est un manque d'imagination.
~ Despair is a lack of imagination.

—Georges Dumézil

---

* See also ORIGINAL SIN, same author.

~ The worst is not, so long we can say: this is the worst.

—SHAKESPEARE

~ The mass of men lead lives of quiet desperation.

—THOREAU

DEVIL

On n'a jamais rien dit ni écrit qui aille si loin que les paroles du diable au Christ dans saint Luc concernant les royaumes du monde: 'Je te donnerai toute cette puissance et la gloire qui y est attachée car elle m'a été abandonée, à moi et à tout être à qui je veux en faire part.' Il en résulte que le social est irréductiblement le domaine du diable.

~ No words, no writing ever went further than what the Devil said to Jesus in Luke's Gospel about the kingdoms of this world: 'I will give you command over all these, and the glory that belongs to them; they have been made over to me, and I may give them to whomsoever I please.' Consequently, society is irreducibly the Devil's domain.

—SIMONE WEIL

Étonnantes jocrisseries des occultes (!) qui ont besoin de rites et de grimoires pour sentir la présence du Démon, et

qui ne voient pas le Satanisme – à crever les yeux – de
leur épicier, par exemple.

~ Stupendous stupidity of the disciples of the 'occult',
who need rituals and mumbo-jumbo to feel the presence of the Devil – but who do not see the Satanism,
right before their eyes, of their grocer.

—LÉON BLOY

Tout, dans ce monde, est inexplicable sans l'intervention
du Démon. Ceux qui se souviennent habituellement de
cet Ennemi peuvent entrevoir, avec autant d'admiration
que de crainte, le dessous des choses.

~ Everything in this world is inexplicable without taking into account the Devil's intervention. Those who
are constantly aware of the existence of this Enemy are
able to glimpse with awe and fear the hidden underside
of things.

—LÉON BLOY

~ Of all bad men, religious bad men are the worst. Of
all created beings, the wickedest is the one who stood
in the immediate presence of God.

—C. S. LEWIS

~ In the Gospels, it was the Devil who first recog-
nised Christ, and the Evangelists did not censor this

information. They apparently thought it was pretty good witness.

—FLANNERY O'CONNOR

DISTANCE

La distance est l'âme de la beauté.
~ Distance is the soul of beauty.

—SIMONE WEIL

La magie des lointains, cette partie de la peinture qui attache les imaginations tendres est peut-être la principale cause de sa supériorité sur la sculpture. Par là, elle se rapproche de la musique […] Les sentiments divins ne peuvent exister ici-bas qu'autant qu'ils durent peu.
~ The magic of distant horizons, that part of painting which seduces tender imaginations, is perhaps the main reason for its superiority over sculpture. In this respect, painting is akin to music […] Divine feelings can exist in this world only in so far as they do not last.

—STENDHAL

~ When I was ten or eleven, it occurred to me that Marx's dictum that 'existence conditions consciousness' was true only for as long as it takes consciousness to

acquire the art of estrangement; thereafter consciousness is on its own and can both condition and ignore
existence.

—JOSEPH BRODSKY

DISTRACTION

*J'aime les gens distraits; c'est une marque qu'ils ont des
idées et qu'ils sont bons; car les méchants et les sots ont
toujours de la présence d'esprit.*

~ I love absent-minded people; absent-mindedness is
the mark of a man who has ideas and who is kind; for
the evil-minded and the blockhead always have their
wits about them.

—PRINCE DE LIGNE

DOING GOOD

*Faire seulement, en fait d'actes de vertu, ceux dont on ne
peut pas s'empêcher, ceux qu'on ne peut pas ne pas faire,
mais augmenter sans cesse par l'attention bien dirigée la
quantité de ceux qu'on ne peut pas ne pas faire.*

~ As regards virtuous deeds, do only those actions
which you are irresistibly impelled to do, which you
cannot not do. However, through well directed attention, constantly increase the number of actions which
you are irresistibly impelled to do.

—SIMONE WEIL

~ You must have a genius for charity as well as for anything else. As for Doing-good, that is one of the professions which are full. Moreover I have tried it fairly, and, strange as it may seem, am satisfied that it does not agree with my constitution […] There is no odour so bad as that which arises from goodness tainted. It is human, it is divine, carrion. If I knew for a certainty that a man was coming to my house with the conscious design of doing me good, I should run for my life.

—THOREAU

DREAM

Rompre avec les choses réelles, ce n'est rien. Mais avec les souvenirs! Le cœur se brise à la séparation des songes, tant il y a peu de réalité dans l'homme.

~ To relinquish real things is easy enough. As for memories, however, they are another matter altogether: what breaks our heart is to be parted from our dreams – for there is so little reality within man.

—CHATEAUBRIAND

ECONOMY

~ The only thing that can console one for being poor is extravagance; the only thing that can console one for being rich is economy.

—OSCAR WILDE

EPITAPH

~ Under the wide and starry sky
Dig the grave and let me lie;
Glad did I live and gladly die,
And I laid me down with a will.
This be the verse you grave for me:
Here he lies where he longed to be,
Home is the sailor, home from sea
And the hunter home from the hill.

—R. L. STEVENSON

~ After I am dead, I wish it may be said
His sins were scarlet but his books were read.

—HILAIRE BELLOC

FAILURE

~ Success is the necessary misfortune of human life,
but it is only to the very unfortunate that it comes early.

—TROLLOPE

~ It is a rule of God's Providence that we succeed by
failure.

—JOHN HENRY NEWMAN

~ Success alters people, while failure reveals them
really as they are.

—BRIAN MOORE

FAITH

~ I think there is no suffering greater than what is caused by the doubts of those who want to believe. I know what torment this is, but I can only see it, in myself anyway, as the process by which faith is deepened. A faith that just accepts is a child's faith and all right for children, but eventually you have to grow religiously as every other way, though some never do. What people don't realise is how much religion costs. They think faith is a large electric blanket, when of course it is the cross.

—Flannery O'Connor

Mon père, incroyant, me disait: 'Tu ne crois guère, les catholiques croient peu. Si je croyais à l'Eucharistie – Dieu sur Terre, y penses-tu! Dieu! – rien d'autre ne me serait plus au monde. Seuls, les moines ont la foi. Seuls, ils sont logiques. Seuls, ils sont dans le vrai de leur vérité.'

~ My father, a non-believer, used to tell me: 'You have so little faith. Catholics have so little faith. If only I could believe in the Eucharist! – God on earth, think of it! God! Nothing else would matter any more for me in this world. Only monks have faith. Only monks are consistent. They alone are true to their truth.'

—Marie Noël

FICTION

Le fait que l'existence n'est pas un bien contraint l'homme, qui ne peut pas se passer de bien, à vivre dans l'imaginaire, c'est-à-dire dans le faux. L'obéissance seule le délivre de cette contrainte. Elle permet seule de supporter le présent.

~ The fact that existence is not a good in itself obliges man, who cannot do without good, to live in an imaginary world – which is to say, in a realm of falsehood. Only obedience can free him from this constraint. Obedience alone enables one to bear actuality.

—SIMONE WEIL

~ Novels arise out of the shortcomings of history.

—NOVALIS

FIDELITY

La fidélité est un des signes du génie.
~ Fidelity is one of the marks of genius.

—BAUDELAIRE

FIRST PRINCIPLES

~ Nothing that really matters can be either proved or disproved.

—UNAMUNO

~ Fundamental perceptions are intuitive and unarguable; all important truths, whether of physics or ethics, must at last be self-evident.

—Emerson

~ The chief fallacy is to believe that truth is a result which comes at the end of a thought-process. Truth on the contrary is always the beginning of thought, thinking is always result-less [...] Thinking starts after an experience of truth has struck home, so to speak [...] Truth, in other words, is not 'in' thought, but (to use Kant's language) the condition for the possibility of thinking. It is both beginning and a priori.

—Hannah Arendt

FLEA

Être petit et s'attaquer à quelqu'un de très grand est une action d'éclat. C'est beau d'être la puce d'un lion [...] Le lion humilié a dans sa chair le dard de l'insecte, et la puce peut dire: j'ai en moi du sang de lion.

~ To be tiny and yet to attack someone very big is a brilliant feat. It is glorious to be a flea on a lion [...] The humiliated lion carries in its flesh the sting of the insect, and the flea can say: I have lion's blood in me.

—Victor Hugo

FRIENDS

Dans le monde, vous avez trois sortes d'amis: vos amis qui vous aiment, vos amis qui ne se soucient pas de vous, et vos amis qui vous haïssent.

~ In society, you have three kinds of friends: those friends who love you, those friends who do not care for you, and those friends who hate you.

—CHAMFORT

Un ami n'est pas plus méchant qu'un autre homme.
~ A friend is no worse than any other man.

—ALFRED DE VIGNY

GENTLEMAN

~ It is almost a definition of a gentleman that he never inflicts pain.

—JOHN HENRY NEWMAN

On ne s'imagine Platon et Aristote qu'avec de grandes robes de pédants. C'étaient des gens honnêtes et, comme les autres, riant avec leurs amis; et aussi quand ils se sont divertis à faire leurs Lois et leurs Politique, ils l'ont fait en se jouant; c'était la partie la moins philosophe et la moins sérieuse de leur vie, la plus philosophe était de vivre simplement et tranquillement. S'ils ont écrit de politique, c'était comme pour régler un hôpital de fous; et s'ils ont fait semblant d'en parler comme d'une grande chose, c'est qu'ils savaient que les fous à qui ils parlaient pensaient être rois et empereurs. Ils entrent dans leurs principes pour modérer leur folie au moins mal qu'il se peut.

~ We always picture Plato and Aristotle in solemn academic gowns. But they were gentlemen, and as such, used to enjoy a laugh with their friends, and when they amused themselves by composing their *Laws* and *Politics*, they did it for fun; actually it was the least philosophical and serious part of their activity; the most philosophical part was to live simply and quietly. If they wrote about politics, it was as if to lay down rules for a madhouse. And if they pretended to treat it as something very important, it was because they knew that the madmen they were talking to believed themselves to be kings and emperors. They humoured these beliefs only in order to constrain the madness as well as they could.

—PASCAL

GOAL

~ In the long run, men hit only what they aim at. Therefore though they should fail immediately, they had better aim at something high.

—THOREAU

GOD

Vocatus atque non vocatus deus aderit.

~ Whether you call for him or not, God will be there.

—DELPHIC ORACLE TO THE LACEDEMONIANS BEFORE A BATTLE AGAINST ATHENS. INSCRIPTION ABOVE THE DOOR OF C. G. JUNG.

Nada te turbe,
Nada te espante,
Todo se pasa,
Dios no se muda.
La paciencia
Todo lo alcanza.
Quien a Dios tiene
Nada le falta.
Solo Dios basta.

~ Let nothing trouble you,
Let nothing scare you,
All is floating,
God alone is unchanging.
Patience
Everything obtains.
Who possesses God
Nothing wants.
God alone suffices.

—SAINT TERESA OF AVILA

Sufro yo a tu costa
Dios no existente, pues si Tú existieras
Existiría yo tambien de veras.
~ I suffer at your expense
Non-existing God, for if you were to exist
Me too, I would truly exist.

—UNAMUNO

Les Juifs et les Chrétiens, liseurs charnels d'un Livre
effroyablement symbolique, vivent tous, depuis quarante
siècles, sur l'illusion d'un Dieu magnifique et omnipo-
tent. Je pense au contraire qu'il faut tout quitter, tout
vendre, pour faire l'aumône à ce Seigneur qui ne pos-
sède rien, qui ne peut rien, qui est infirme de tous ses
membres, qui sent très mauvais, qui se racle sur tous les
fumiers de l'Orient ou de l'Occident, et crie d'angoisse
depuis les éternités, en attendant le Carillon du Sep-
tième Jour.

C'est pour cela que j'exècre les triomphants et les déli-
cats.

~ Jews and Christians, carnal readers of a frightfully
symbolical Book, have all lived for the last forty centu-
ries under the illusion that God must be splendid and
all-powerful. I believe on the contrary that one should
forsake everything, *sell* everything, to give alms to this
Lord who owns nothing, who is totally crippled, who

stinks, who scratches himself on all the manure-heaps of the East and the West, and who cries in anguish from the beginning of time, waiting for the Carillon of the Seventh Day.

That is why I loathe the triumphant and the delicate.

—Léon Bloy

Pas de nouvelles de Dieu.
~ No news from God.

—Léon Bloy

Entre deux hommes qui n'ont pas l'expérience de Dieu, celui qui le nie en est peut-être le plus près.
~ Of two men who have no experience of God, the one who denies him is perhaps the closest to him.

—Simone Weil

Dieu existe. Dieu n'existe pas. Où est le problème? Je suis tout à fait sûre qu'il y a un Dieu, en ce sens que je suis tout à fait sûre que mon amour n'est pas illusoire. Je suis tout à fait sûre qu'il n'y a pas de Dieu, en ce sens que je suis tout à fait sûre que rien de réel ne ressemble à ce que je peux concevoir quand je prononce ce nom. Mais cela que je ne peux pas concevoir n'est pas une illusion.

~ God exists. God does not exist. Where is the problem? I am absolutely certain that there is a God, in the sense that I am absolutely certain that my love is not an illusion. I am absolutely certain that there is no God, in the sense that I am absolutely certain that there is nothing real which corresponds to what I can think of when I pronounce this name. Yet that which I cannot think of is not an illusion.

—SIMONE WEIL

~ Happy, intense absorption in any work, which is to be brought as near to perfection as possible, this is a state of being with God, and the men who have not known it have missed life itself.

—D. H. LAWRENCE

Que doit penser Dieu quant il lit un traité de théologie? Mais Dieu ne sait pas lire.
~ What must God think when he reads a theological treatise? But God cannot read.

—MARIE NOËL

~ When a man stops believing in God, he doesn't then believe in nothing – he believes in anything.

—CHESTERTON

GRASS

~ A philosopher always finds more grass to feed upon in the valleys of stupidity than on the arid heights of intelligence.

—WITTGENSTEIN

GREATNESS

Je suis insatiable des connaissances qui peuvent me faire grand; je me rappelle, en m'y conformant par une pente toute naturelle, ce que m'écrivait Beyle: 'Ne négligez rien de ce qui peut vous faire grand.'

~ I always thirst for any knowledge that can help me to achieve greatness. I remember, and I follow by natural inclination, what Beyle once wrote to me: 'Neglect nothing that can make you great.'*

—DELACROIX

HAPPINESS

~ Bliss was it in that dawn to be alive
But to be young was very heaven.

—WORDSWORTH

---

* This advice from his friend Beyle (Stendhal) struck Delacroix deeply. He recalls it several times in his *Journal*.

Être avec les gens qu'on aime, cela suffit, rêver, leur parler, ne leur parler point, penser à eux, penser à des choses plus indifférentes, mais auprès d'eux, tout est égal.

~ To be with those we love – that is enough; we may dream, or we may talk to them, or not talk to them, think of them, or think of more indifferent things: as long as we are close to them, nothing really matters.

—LA BRUYÈRE

Le bonheur n'est pas chose aisée. Il est très difficile de le trouver en nous, et impossible de le trouver ailleurs.

~ Happiness is not an easy matter. It is difficult to find it in ourselves and impossible to find it anywhere else.

—CHAMFORT

Que chacun examine ce qu'il a souhaité toute sa vie. S'il est heureux, c'est parce que ses vœux n'ont point été exaucés.

~ Let each one examine what he has desired all his life. If he is happy, it is because his wishes have not been granted.

—PRINCE DE LIGNE

HELL

~ Hell is truth seen too late.

—HOBBES

~ Hell is what God's love becomes to those who reject it. If there were no hell, we would be like the animals. No hell, no dignity.

—FLANNERY O'CONNOR

~ Only the Self burns in Hell.

—MASTER ECKHART

HISTORY

Tout a toujours très mal marché.
~ Everything has always worked out very badly.

—JACQUES BAINVILLE

~ The past is not dead, it is not even past.

—FAULKNER

L'histoire ne retient pas les faits, elle ne retient que leur écho.
~ History does not record facts, it only records their echoes.

—HENRI PIRENNE

HOMOSEXUALITY

Il paraît que beaucoup de directeurs de théâtre sont homosexuels. Cela me rappelle mon cousin Bedon qui est marchand de vin et qui ne veut boire que du cidre.

~ I am told that many theatre directors are homosexual. This reminds me of my cousin Bedon, who is a wine merchant and only drinks cider.

—PAUL CLAUDEL

HOUSE

C'est une des tristesses de la civilisation que d'habiter dans des maisons. Je crois que nous sommes faits pour nous endormir sur le dos en regardant les étoiles. Dans quelques années, l'humanité (par le développement nouveau de la locomotion) va revenir à son état nomade. On voyagera d'un bout du monde à l'autre, comme on faisait autrefois, de la prairie à la montagne: cela remettra du calme dans les esprits et de l'air dans les poumons.

~ One of the sorrows of civilisation is that we must live in houses. I do believe that we were meant to sleep lying on our backs and looking at the stars. In a few years (because of new developments in transportation) mankind will revert to its nomadic state. We will travel all over the world as people used to do in the past, from pastures to mountains: it will restore peace of mind and put air back into our lungs.

—FLAUBERT

~ I have sometimes thought that a woman's nature is like a great house full of rooms: there is the hall through which everyone passes going in and out, the drawing room where one receives formal visits, the sitting room where members of the family come and go as they wish; but beyond that, far beyond, there are other rooms, the handles of whose doors are never turned […] I believe I know the only cure [for restoring inner peace], which is to make one's centre of life inside of one's self, not selfishly or excludingly, but with a kind of unassailable serenity, to decorate one's inner house so richly that one is content there.

—EDITH WHARTON

~ A house of which one knows every room is not worth living in.

—LAMPEDUSA

HUMANISM

Homo fit non nascitur.
~ One is not born a man, one becomes a man.

—ERASMUS

Humanum paucis vivit genus.
~ Mankind survives thanks to a few.

—JULIUS CAESAR

I

~ I should not talk so much about myself if there were anybody else whom I knew so well.

—Thoreau

Nous ne possédons rien au monde – car le hasard peut tout nous ôter – sinon le pouvoir de dire je. *C'est cela qu'il faut donner à Dieu, c'est-à-dire détruire. Il n'y a absolument aucun autre acte libre qui nous soit permis, sinon la destruction du* je.

~ We own nothing in this world, for chance may always take everything away – except the power to say 'I'. And it is this which we give to God – in other words, this which we must destroy. We are allowed absolutely no other free action, except this destruction of 'I'.

—Simone Weil

ILLUSION

~ Every age is fed on illusions, lest men should renounce life early and the human race come to an end.

—Conrad

IMITATION, BORROWING

~ As soon as a thing gives me pleasure, it becomes mine, whatever its origin may be.

—RABINDRANATH TAGORE

~ We all steal, but in the end we are judged on who we stole from, and what we did with it.

—MARTHA GRAHAM

~ Immature poets imitate, mature poets steal.

—T. S. ELIOT

~ The greatest genius will never be worth much if he pretends to draw exclusively on his own resources [...] What is genius but the faculty of seizing and turning to account anything that strikes us [...] Every one of my writings has been furnished to me by a thousand different persons, a thousand different things [...] My work is an aggregation of things taken from the whole of Nature: it bears the name of Goethe.

—GOETHE

INTELLECTUALS

Nihil tam absurdum dici potest quod non dicatur ab aliquo philosophorum.

~ One cannot think of any absurdity so extreme, that some philosopher would not have uttered it already.

—CICERO

~ You have to be a member of the intelligentsia to believe such a thing – no ordinary man can be such a fool.

—ORWELL

~ An intellectual is a person knowledgeable in one field who only speaks out in another.

—TOM WOLFE

~ The first moral duty of an intellectual is to be intelligent.

—SIDNEY HOOK

INTELLIGENCE

L'intelligence est caractérisée par une incompréhension naturelle de la vie.
~ Intelligence is characterised by a natural incomprehension of life.

—BERGSON

~ It is not the clear-sighted who lead the world. Great achievements are accomplished in a blessed, warm mental fog.

—CONRAD

Souvent les bêtises ont un sens.
~ Silliness often has a meaning.

—Victor Hugo

L'intelligence n'est pas plus la qualité essentielle d'un artiste que celle d'un militaire n'est la prudence.
~ Intelligence is not an essential quality for an artist, any more than prudence would be for a military man.

—Paul Claudel

INTERVIEW

~ Certain trades and classes seek personal publicity; not so respectable writers, for their entire vocation is one of self-expression and it seems obvious to them that, if they cannot make themselves understood in years of laborious writing, they will not succeed in a few minutes of conversation. So, when we see interviewers advancing, we fly.

—Evelyn Waugh

JEWS

On oublie trop quand on vomit sur les Juifs que le Sauveur lui-même, parlant à la Samaritaine, a dit cette parole [...]: 'Salus ex judaeis est.' On paraît avoir oublié également que toute la liturgie chrétienne est puisée dans les livres juifs, que cette Race, vraiment unique, fut choisie pour donner au genre humain les Patriarches, les Prophètes, les Évangélistes, les Apôtres, les Amis fidèles et tous les premiers martyrs; sans oser parler de la Vierge Mère et de Notre Sauveur lui-même, qui fut le Lion de Juda, le Juif par excellence de nature – un Juif indicible!

Le salut du genre humain est solidaire de la destinée des Juifs.

~ People who make abusive comments about the Jews forget too easily that our Saviour himself, talking to the Samaritan woman, said these words [...]: '*Salus ex Judeais est.*'* They seem also to forget that this race, truly unique, was selected to give mankind the Patriarchs, the Prophets, the Evangelists, the Apostles, the faithful friends and all the first martyrs; and I dare not speak of the Virgin Mother herself, and our Saviour himself, who was the Lion of Judah, sublime Jew, Jew *par excellence*!

The salvation of mankind is inseparable from the destiny of the Jews.

—LÉON BLOY

---

* Salvation comes from the Jews.

JUSTICE

Harmonie sociale – si l'on sait par où la société est déséquilibrée, il faut faire ce qu'on peut pour ajouter du poids dans le plateau trop léger [...] Mais il faut avoir conçu l'équilibre et être toujours prêt à changer de côté, comme la justice, 'cette fugitive du camp des vainqueurs'.

~ Social harmony – if one knows where society has lost balance, one must endeavour to add weight to the lighter scale [...] But one must keep in mind the point of equilibrium, and remain forever ready to shift to the other side, like justice, 'this fugitive from the camp of victory'.

—SIMONE WEIL

KNOWLEDGE

知之為知之。不知為不知。是知也。

論語

~ To take what you know for what you know, and what you do not know for what you do not know, that is knowledge indeed.

—ANALECTS OF CONFUCIUS

~ Men more often require to be reminded than in-formed.

—SAMUEL JOHNSON

人皆求其所未知。而不知求其所巳知.

莊子

~ People all seek to know what they do not know yet; they ought rather seek to know what they know already.

—ZHUANG ZI

Je ne comprends que ce que je devine.
~ I only understand what I guess.

—LÉON BLOY

~ The highest we can attain is not knowledge, but sympathy with intelligence.

—THOREAU

LAUGHTER

La plus perdue de toutes les journées est celle où l'on n'a pas ri.
~ The most wasted of all days is a day without laughter.

—CHAMFORT

LEISURE, LAZINESS*

Il faut en France beaucoup de fermeté et une grande étendue d'esprit pour se passer des charges et des emplois, et consentir ainsi à demeurer chez soi et à ne rien faire: personne presque n'a assez de mérite pour jouer ce rôle avec dignité, ni assez de fond pour remplir le vide du temps sans ce que le vulgaire appelle les affaires. Il ne manque cependant à l'oisiveté du sage qu'un meilleur nom, et que méditer, parler, lire et être tranquille s'appelât travailler.

~ In France you need great inner strength and vast learning to do without official position or employment, and simply stay home, doing nothing; almost no one has sufficient character to do this with dignity, or to fill their days without what is commonly called 'business'. And yet the only thing that the wise man's leisure lacks is a better name: meditation, conversation, reading and inner peace should be called 'work'.

—LA BRUYÈRE

~ No, sir, I am not obliged to do any more. No man is obliged to do as much as he can do. A man is to have part of his life for himself.

—SAMUEL JOHNSON

---

* See also WORK.

~ All intellectual improvement arises from leisure.

—SAMUEL JOHNSON

~ I hold that happiness is impossible without idleness. My ideal is to be idle and love a fat girl.

—CHEKHOV

Je suis fait pour une paresse intelligente.
~ I was made for intelligent sloth.

—ABBÉ MUGNIER

J'ai tellement besoin de temps pour ne rien faire, qu'il ne m'en reste plus pour travailler.
~ I need so much time to do nothing that I have no time left for work.

—P. REVERDY

LIE

~ I believe that while we are alive we lie to protect ourselves from the truth itself. The lies we tell are part of the life we live, and therefore part of the truth.

—BERNARD SHAW

LIFE

人生到處知何似。應似飛鴻踏雪泥。
泥上偶然留指爪。鴻飛那復計東西。
老僧已死成新塔。壞壁無由見舊題。
往日崎嶇還記否。路長人困蹇驢嘶。

蘇軾

~ To what should we compare human life? It should
be compared to a wild goose trampling on the snow.
The snow retains for a moment the imprint of its feet;
the goose flies away no one knows where.

Our friend, the old monk, has died; on the ruined
wall of the monastery the poem we wrote the other
year has become illegible. Do you still remember our
past adventures and tribulations?

The road is long, the traveller is tired, his limping
donkey brays.

—SU DONGPO

*Qui de nous n'a eu sa Terre promise, son jour d'extase et
sa fin en exil?*
~ Which one of us did not have his Promised Land,
his day of ecstasy and his end in exile?

—AMIEL

~ Life is like playing a violin solo in public, and learning the instrument as one goes on.

—SAMUEL BUTLER

Ô l'infernale disgrâce de subsister sans groin dans un monde sans Dieu!
~ O, the hellish disgrace of having to survive without a snout in a world without God!

—LÉON BLOY

~ I wonder if there is anyone who feels ashamed, among all those who have built their comfortable, secure, upright academic careers on the life of a poet who lived in misery and despair.

—CANETTI

~ A man's life is his whole life, not the last glimmering snuff of the candle.

—HAZLITT

De ma vie, je n'ai jamais rien vu qui fût laid.
~ In all my life I never saw anything that was ugly.

—CLAUDE MONET

~ When one subtracts from life infancy, sleep, eating and swilling, buttoning and unbuttoning – how much remains of downright existence? The summer of a dormouse.

—BYRON

~ Maybe an unexamined life is not worth living. But a man's examined life can make him wish he was dead.

—SAUL BELLOW

Cette vie est un hôpital où chaque malade est possédé du désir de changer de lit. Celui-ci voudrait souffrir en face du poêle, et celui-là croit qu'il guérirait à côté de la fenêtre.
~ Life is a hospital where every patient wishes to be moved to another bed. This one wants to suffer in front of the stove, and that one believes he would get well next to the window.

—BAUDELAIRE

La vie a un goût de bonheur comme les roses ont une odeur de rose.
~ Life tastes of happiness, in the same way that roses smell of rose.

—J. PAULHAN

La vie est un rondeau; elle finit à peu près comme elle a commencé; les deux enfances en sont une preuve. Il n'y a que l'intervalle chez chacun qui soit différent.

~ Life is a rondeau: it ends more or less as it began – its two infancies prove this. The only difference is the interval between them.

—PRINCE DE LIGNE

LIFE DRAWING

~ I found myself lying on the bank of a cart-road in the sand, with no prospect whatever but that small aspen tree against the blue sky. Languidly but not idly, I began to draw it; and as I drew, the languor passed away: the beautiful lines insisted on being traced – without weariness. More and more beautiful they became, as each rose out of the rest, and took its place in the air. With wonder increasing every instant, I saw that they 'composed' themselves by finer laws than any known of men. At last the tree was there and anything that I had thought about trees, nowhere.

—RUSKIN

LIMIT

~ For a long time now I have been of the view (an opinion increasingly neglected, if not mocked, by newspapers, television and even literature) that there should be an insuperable limit placed on what can be told to all men on the subject of Man.

—GUSTAV HERLING

LITERATURE

La littérature, ce n'est pas (malgré l'apparence) quelque chose de sensé que l'on teinte d'un peu de folie. C'est le contraire: une sorte de folie que l'on rend à peu près vrai- semblable.

~ Literature is not (in spite of appearances) something reasonable to which one adds a touch of madness. It is the opposite: a sort of madness which one endeavours to make more or less plausible.

—J. PAULHAN

~ Without literature, human life is animal life.

—RANDALL JARRELL

~ Nothing is important except the fate of the soul – and literature is only redeemed from an utter trivial- ity surpassing that of noughts and crosses, by the fact that it describes not the world around us, or the things on the retina of the eye, or the enormous irrelevance of Encyclopaedias, but some condition to which the human spirit can come. All good writers express the state of their souls, even (as occurs in some cases of very good writers) if it is a state of damnation.

—CHESTERTON

~ A work that aspires, however humbly, to the condition of art, should carry its justification in every line. And art itself may be defined as a single minded attempt to render the highest kind of justice to the visible universe, by bringing to light the truth, manifold and one, underlying its every aspect.

—CONRAD

Ce qui me semble à moi le plus haut dans l'art (et le plus difficile), ce n'est pas de faire rire, ni de faire pleurer, ni de vous mettre en rut ou en fureur, mais d'agir à la façon de la nature, c'est-à-dire de faire rêver. Aussi les très belles œuvres ont ce caractère. Elles sont sereines d'aspect et incompréhensibles. Quant au procédé, elles sont immobiles comme des falaises, houleuses comme l'océan, pleines de frondaisons, de verdures et de murmures comme des bois, tristes comme le désert, bleues comme le ciel. Homère, Rabelais, Michel-Ange, Shakespeare, Goethe m'apparaissent impitoyables. Cela est sans fond, infini,

multiple. Par de petites ouvertures, on aperçoit des préci-
pices; il y a du noir en bas, du vertige. Et cependant
quelque chose de singulièrement doux plane sur l'ensem-
ble! C'est l'éclat de la lumière, le sourire du soleil, et c'est
calme! c'est calme! et c'est fort, ça a des fanons comme le
bœuf de Leconte [de Lisle].

~ What seems to me the highest achievement of art
(and the most difficult) is not to make you laugh, or to
make you cry, nor to arouse your lust or excite your
anger, but to operate like nature – which is to *make*
you dream. Thus all the most beautiful works present
this character; their outlook is serene and incomprehensible; as to their method: they are immobile like
cliffs, turbulent like the ocean, full of deep, green,
murmuring foliages like a forest, sad as the desert, blue
as the sky. Homer, Rabelais, Michelangelo, Shakespeare, Goethe all seem *ruthless* to me. They are
unfathomable, infinite, many sided. They afford sud-
den glimpses into abysses – deep down it is dark and
vertiginous, and yet a strange sweetness bathes it all!
It has the brilliance of light, the smile of the sun, and
it is calm! so calm! and powerful like a huge and majes-
tic ox.

—Flaubert

~ Literature enlarges our being by admitting us to experiences not our own. They may be beautiful, terrible, awe-inspiring, exhilarating, pathetic, comic, or merely piquant. Literature gives the *entrée* to them all. Those of us who have been true readers all our life seldom fully realise the enormous extension of our being which we owe to authors. We realise it best when we talk with an unliterary friend. He may be full of goodness and good sense, but he inhabits a tiny world. In it, we should be suffocated. The man who is contented to be only himself, and therefore less a self, is in prison. My own eyes are not enough for me … Even the eyes of all humanity are not enough. I regret that the brutes cannot write books. Very gladly would I learn what face things present to a mouse or a bee, more gladly still would I perceive the olfactory world charged with all the information and emotion it carries for a dog. In reading good literature, I become a thousand men, and yet remain myself. Like the night sky in the Greek poem, I see with a myriad eyes, but it is still I who see. Here, as in worship, in love, in moral action, and in knowing, I transcend myself; and I am never more myself than when I do.

— C. S. Lewis

Il semble que la littérature ne soit pas une fin en soi que l'on se proposerait, mais l'accompagnement, mais la fleur d'autre chose.

~ Literature, it seems, cannot be an end in itself, or a goal one would set for oneself; on the contrary, it is the accompaniment, the flower of something else.

—J. PAULHAN

LITOTES

少年不識愁滋味
愛上層樓愛上層樓
為賦新詞強説愁
而今識盡愁滋味
欲説还休欲説还休
却道天凉好个秋

辛棄疾

~ In my youth, I did not know the taste of sorrow, but I enjoyed climbing to high balconies, and there, to sing new songs, I would contrive imaginary sorrows. Today, having tasted sorrow to the full, I wish to speak – and yet I refrain, and just say: The air is cool, what a lovely autumn!

—XIN QIJI

~ Jesus, there is but one art: to omit! O if I knew how to omit, I would ask no other knowledge. A man who knew how to omit would make an Iliad out of a daily paper.

—R. L. Stevenson

Le secret d'ennuyer c'est de tout dire.
~ The secret of being a bore is to say everything.

—Voltaire

意達筆不到

~ The meaning is fully expressed without the brush having to run its full course.

—anonymous

Stendhal est pénétré de ce grand principe: malheur en amour comme dans les arts à qui dit tout.
~ Stendhal is deeply aware of this great principle: woe, in love as in art, to him who tells everything!

—Balzac

LOVE

~ The closest human love encloses a potential germ of estrangement or hatred.

—William James

~ For the man who loves much – I mean love for a woman – love occupies in his life a subordinate or secondary position, whereas it is everything for he who loves little.

—UNAMUNO

~ We can do no great things, only small things with great love.

—MOTHER TERESA

MADNESS

~ Of the uncertainties of our present state, one of the most dreadful and alarming is the uncertain continuance of reason.

—SAMUEL JOHNSON

MARRIAGE

~ Love is temporary and ends with marriage. Marriage is the perfection love aimed at, ignorant of what is sought. Marriage is a good known only to the parties. A relation of perfect understanding, aid, contentment, possession of themselves, and of the world – which dwarfs love to green fruit.

—EMERSON

~ Levin had been married three months. He was happy, but not at all in the way he had expected to be. At every step he found his former dreams disappointed, and now, unexpected surprises of happiness. He was happy, but on entering family life, he saw at every step that it was utterly different from what he had imagined. At every step, he experienced what a man would experience who, after admiring the smooth, happy course of a little boat on a lake, should get himself into that little boat. He saw that it was not all sitting still, floating smoothly, that one had to think too, not for an instant to forget where one was floating, and that there was water under one, and that one must row; and that his unaccustomed hands would be sore, and that it was only to look at that was easy; but doing, though very delightful, was very difficult.

—TOLSTOY

~ Of all human institutions, marriage is the one which most depends upon slow development, upon patience, upon long reaches of time, upon magnanimous compromise, upon kindly habit [...] As to that dreamy old bachelor notion – the notion that the unity of marriage, the being one flesh, has something to do with being perfectly happy, or being perfectly good, or even with being perfectly and continuously affection-ate – I tell you, an ordinary, honest man is part of his wife even when he wishes he wasn't. I tell you, an ordinary good woman is part of her husband, even when she wishes him at the bottom of the sea. I tell you that, whether the two people are for the moment friendly or angry, happy or unhappy, the thing marches on, the great four-footed thing, the quadruped of the home. They are a nation, a society, a machine. I tell you, they are one flesh when they are not one spirit.

—Chesterton

MASK

~ Man is least himself when he talks in his own person. Give him a mask, and he will tell you the truth.

—Oscar Wilde

~ Every profound spirit needs a mask; even more, around every profound spirit, a mask is growing continually, owing to the constantly false, namely *shallow* interpretation of every word, every step, every sign of life he gives.

—Nietzsche

MASS

~ We pray in silence. 'Participation' in the Mass does not mean hearing our own voices. It means God hearing our voices. Only He knows who is 'participating' at Mass. I believe, to compare small things with great, that I 'participate' in a work of art when I study it and love it silently [...] I am now old, but I was young when I was received into the Church. I was not at all attracted by the splendour of her great ceremonies – which the Protestants could well counterfeit. Of the extraneous attractions of the Church which most drew me was the spectacle of the priest and his server at Low Mass, stumping up to the altar without a glance to discover how many or how few he had in his congregation, a craftsman and his apprentice; a man with a job which he alone was qualified to do. That is the Mass I have grown to know and love. By all means let the rowdy have their 'dialogues', but let us who value silence not be completely forgotten.

—EVELYN WAUGH

MEMORY*

~ Imagination is the morning, memory the evening of the mind.

The rule is that for every fact added to the memory, one is crowded out, and that only what the affection animates can be remembered.

Inventive people have bad memories.

—EMERSON

De toutes les facultés humaines, le mémoire paraît la plus ruinée par la Chute. Une preuve bien certaine de l'infirmité de notre mémoire, c'est notre ignorance de l'avenir.

~ Of all the human faculties, memory seems to have suffered most from the Fall. A clear evidence of this impairment of our memory is provided by our ignorance of the future.

—LÉON BLOY

MIND AND HEART

Il faut avoir l'esprit dur et le cœur tendre. Mais le monde est plein de cœurs secs à l'esprit mou.

---

* See also PROUST.

~ One must have a hard mind and a tender heart. Yet the world is full of dry hearts with soft brains.

—J. MARITAIN

MISANTHROPY

Si vous me demandez quelles sont les épreuves qu'il a dû traverser, je ne serai pas en mesure de vous répondre. Tout ce que je peux vous dire, c'est que l'impression qu'il donne est de quelqu'un de blessé, *à l'égal, suis-je tenté d'ajouter, de tous ceux à qui fut refusé le don de l'illusion. Ne redoutez pas de le rencontrer: de tous les êtres, les moins insupportables sont ceux qui haïssent les hommes. Il ne faut jamais fuir un misanthrope.*

~ If you ask me what sort of trials he went through, I shall not be able to tell. All I know is that he looks *wounded*, like all those to whom the gift of illusion was denied. Don't be afraid to meet him; of all creatures, the least unpleasant are those who hate men. Never run away from a misanthrope.

—CIORAN

MONEY

~ It takes a certain competence to make money – but it takes culture to spend it.

—MORAVIA

MULTICULTURALISM

~ Who is the Tolstoy of the Zulus? The Proust of the Papuans? I'll be glad to read him.

— SAUL BELLOW

MUSIC

~ The purpose of art is not the release of a momentary ejection of adrenaline, but it is, rather, the gradual, life-long construction of a state of wonder and serenity […] Art on its loftiest mission is scarcely human at all.

— GLENN GOULD

MYSTERY

~ Where there is no mystery, there is no truth.

— B. BRECHT

~ [Letter to Robert Bridges] You do not mean by mystery what a Catholic does. You mean an *interesting uncertainty*: the uncertainty ceasing, interest ceases also. This happens in some things; to you, in religion. But a Catholic by mystery means an *incomprehensible certainty*; without certainty, without formulation, there is no interest […] The clearer the formulation, the greater the interest. At bottom, the source of interest is the same in both cases, in your mind and in ours; it is the unknown, the reserve of truth beyond what the mind reaches and still feels to be behind. But the interest a Catholic feels is, if I may say so, of a far finer kind than yours.

—G. Manley Hopkins

On dégrade les mystères de la foi en en faisant un objet d'affirmation ou de négation, alors qu'ils doivent être un objet de contemplation.

~ One debases the mysteries of faith by treating them as objects for affirmation or negation. They are objects for contemplation.

—Simone Weil

Tous les gens gagnent à être connus. Ils gagnent en mystère.

~ All people gain from being better known. They gain in mystery.

—J. Paulhan

MYTH

~ What flows in you from the myth is not the truth, but reality. Truth is always about something, but reality is what truth is about.

—C. S. Lewis

~ Man's estrangement from the mythical realm, and the subsequent shrinking of his existence to the merely factual – that is the major cause of mental illness.

—C. G. JUNG

NEWSPAPERS

Tout journal, de la première ligne à la dernière, n'est qu'un tissu d'horreurs. Guerres, crimes, vols, impudici- tés, tortures, crimes des princes, crimes des nations, cri- mes des particuliers, une ivresse d'atrocité universelle. Et c'est de ce dégoûtant apéritif que l'homme civilisé accom- pagne son repas de chaque matin. Tout en ce monde sue le crime: le journal, la muraille et le visage de l'homme. Je ne comprends pas qu'une main pure puisse toucher un journal sans une convulsion de dégoût.

~ Every newspaper, from the first line to the last, is nothing but a patchwork of horrors. Wars, crimes, thiev- ery, obscenity, torture, crimes of kings, crimes of nations, crimes of individuals – a universal orgy of atrocities. And it is with such a disgusting cocktail that civilised man washes down his breakfast each morning. Every- thing in this world reeks of crime: newspapers, walls and human faces. I do not understand how a pure hand can touch a newspaper without a spasm of revulsion.

—BAUDELAIRE

Ce que je reproche aux journaux, c'est de nous faire faire attention tous les jours à des choses insignifiantes, tandis que nous lisons trois ou quatre fois dans notre vie des livres où il y a des choses essentielles.

What I reproach newspapers for, is that every day they make us pay attention to insignificant things, whereas, three or four times in all our life, we read books that contain essential things.

—PROUST

NO

Presque tous les hommes sont esclaves par la raison que Les Spartiates donnaient de la servitude des Perses: faute de savoir prononcer la syllabe 'non'. Savoir prononcer ce mot et savoir vivre seul sont les seuls moyens de conserver sa liberté et son caractère.

~ Nearly all men are slaves for the very reason given by the Spartans for the servitude of the Persians: an inability to say the word 'no'. To be able to say 'no' and to be able to live alone are the only two means of preserving one's freedom and one's character.

—CHAMFORT

千人之諾諾不如一士之諤諤．

史記

~ The yes-yes of the crowd carries less weight than the no-no of one decent man.

—SIMA QIAN

NO ABIDING CITY

Non enim habemus hic manentem civitatem, sed futuram inquirimus.
~ Here we have no abiding city, but seek one that is to come.

—SAINT PAUL

OBSCURITY

~ If art is expression, mere clarity is nothing. The extreme clarity of an artist may be due not to his marvellous power of illuminating the abysses of his soul, but merely to the fact that there are no abysses to illuminate […] The impression we receive on first entering the presence of any supreme work of art is obscurity. But it is an obscurity like that of a Catalonian cathedral which slowly grows more luminous as one gazes until the solid structure beneath is revealed.

—HAVELOCK ELLIS

OLD AGE

Les vieillards d'autrefois étaient moins malheureux et moins isolés que ceux d'aujourd'hui: si, en demeurant sur la terre, ils avaient perdu leurs amis, peu de chose du reste avait changé autour d'eux; étrangers à la jeunesse, ils ne l'étaient pas à la société. Maintenant, un traînard dans ce monde a non seulement vu mourir les hommes, mais il a vu mourir les idées: principes, mœurs, goûts, plaisirs, peines, sentiments, rien ne ressemble à ce qu'il a connu. Il est d'une race différente de l'espèce humaine au milieu de laquelle il achève ses jours.

~ In the past old people were not as wretched and lonely as they are today. Staying alive, they lost their friends, but otherwise very little changed around them; in front of the young, they felt like strangers, but they were not strangers within society. Whereas nowadays a laggard in this world has not only witnessed the deaths of men, he has also witnessed the death of ideas: principles, morals, tastes, pleasures, griefs, emotions, nothing remains that resembles what he knew. He ends his days surrounded by men of a different species.

—CHATEAUBRIAND

En tant que vieux, je me supporte, mais je ne supporte pas les vieux – les autres vieux.
~ As an old man I can bear myself, but I cannot bear old people – other old people.

—CIORAN

~ Once, John Whittaker had told me the plot of his favorite science-fiction story. It was a rather sad, nostalgic story about a man of the future, one who is retiring from his position, an important one, at the age of a thousand. I said: 'Did they think he was so old he was about to die, or what?' John answered: 'Oh, no. But they can't use them in jobs any more after they're a thousand: they get too irritable.'

—RANDALL JARRELL

~ Life is first boredom, then fear.

—PHILIP LARKIN

La vieillesse est une voyageuse de la nuit, la terre lui est cachée, elle ne découvre plus que le Ciel.
~ Old age is a traveller of the night: the earth down below has become indistinct, only the sky above can still be seen.

—CHATEAUBRIAND

~ As time goes on you will know yourself better and better. Time does that for you, not only by the increase

76

of experience, but by the withdrawal of those natural assistances to devotion and self-surrender which youth furnishes […] When men get old, as I do, then they see how little grace is in them, and how much what seemed grace was but nature. Then the soul is left to lassitude, torpor, dejection and coldness which is its real state, with no natural impulses, affections or imaginations to rouse it, and things which in youth seemed easy then become difficult. Then it finds how little self-command it has […] Then it understands at length its own nothingness, and that it has less grace than it had, but it has nothing but grace to aid it. It is the sign of a saint to *grow*; common minds, even though they are in the grace of God, dwindle as time goes on. The energy of grace alone can make a soul strong in age.

—JOHN HENRY NEWMAN*

OPINION

Les hommes sont tourmentés par l'opinion qu'ils ont des choses et non par les choses mêmes.
~ What worries people is the opinion they form of things, not the things themselves.

—MONTAIGNE

---

* At the time of writing, Newman was forty-nine – and he was to live another forty years.

OPTIMISM

Le côté infâme de la plupart des philosophies, c'est qu'elles veulent avoir une conclusion optimiste.
~ The infamous aspect of most philosophies is their determination to reach an optimistic conclusion.

—MONTHERLANT

L'optimisme utopique est déprimant et impitoyable. *Je me souviens, par exemple, d'une rencontre avec Teilhard de Chardin: l'homme pérorait avec enthousiasme sur l'évolution du cosmos vers le Christ, le point Oméga, etc. Je lui ai alors demandé ce qu'il pensait de la douleur humaine. 'La douleur et la souffrance, m'a-t-il dit, sont un simple accident de l'évolution.' Je suis parti, indigné, refusant de discuter avec ce débile mental.*
~ Utopian optimism is depressing and *ruthless*. I remember for instance my encounter with Teilhard de Chardin. He was babbling enthusiastically on the cosmic evolution towards Christ, the Omega point, etc. I finally asked him what he thought of human suffering. 'Pain and suffering', he said, 'are simply accidents of evolution.' I left at once, indignant, refusing to converse with someone so mentally defective.

—CIORAN

ORIGINAL SIN

Le marxiste se révolte contre la condition humaine elle-même, c'est-à-dire contre le péché originel. Il prétend organiser le monde comme si le péché originel n'existait pas, ou n'était, comme il le croit, qu'une invention de la classe exploitrice; et il est assurément beaucoup plus grave, ou du moins beaucoup plus dangereux pour l'homme, de nier le péché originel que de nier Dieu.

~ Marxists revolt against the human condition itself, which means against original sin. They endeavour to organise the world as if the Fall never took place, or was only (as they believe) an invention of the exploiting classes. To deny the original sin is certainly much more serious, or at least much more dangerous for man, than to deny God.

—BERNANOS

~ I am a democrat because I believe in the Fall, and therefore think man too wretched to be trusted with more than the minimum power over men.

—C. S. LEWIS

~ Out of the crooked timber of humanity, no straight thing was ever made.

—KANT

PAINTING

Le premier mérite d'un tableau est d'être une fête pour l'œil [...] Tous les yeux ne sont pas propres à goûter les délicatesses de la peinture. Beaucoup ont l'œil faux ou inerte; ils voient littéralement les objets, mais l'exquis, non.

~ The first quality of a painting is to be a feast for the eye [...] All eyes are not able to appreciate the delicate points of painting. Many people have eyes that see 'out of tune' or sluggishly. They may see things in a literal sense, but they do not perceive the exquisite.

—DELACROIX

PARABLE OF KIERKEGAARD

~ Kierkegaard, like Kafka, wrote many religious parables based on contemporary events. One of these was inspired by expeditions to the North Pole and described how Danish clergymen declared in their sermons that participation in such expeditions would help to secure the eternal salvation of the soul. They admitted, however, that it is difficult to reach the Pole, perhaps impossible, and that not everyone is able to undertake such a venture. Eventually they declared that any voyage, for instance from Denmark to London by the regular ferry – or even a Sunday outing in a horse-drawn cab – might count, all things considered, as a genuine expedition to the Pole.

—J. L. Borges

PARABLE OF MULTATULI

~ It was in the evening. A female accosted me. 'Can't you do anything better than sell yourself?' I said, and thrust her away. The next evening, she stood in my way again and thew my *Ideën** in my face. That hurt.

—Multatuli

PARABLE OF SUPERVIELLE

Ma dernière métamorphose.

Soudain je me sentis comblé. J'étais devenu un rhino-céros et trottais dans la brousse. Moi, si vulnérable d'habitude, je pouvais enfin affronter la lutte pour la vie avec de grandes chances de succès. Ma métamorphose me paraissait tout à fait réussie jusqu'en ses profondeurs et tournait au chef-d'œuvre, lorsque j'entendis distincte-ment deux vers de Mallarmé dans ma tête dure et cor-née. Décidément, tout était à recommencer.

~ My last metamorphosis.

Suddenly I experienced total fulfilment. I had turned into a rhinoceros and was trotting through the bush.

---

* His latest book.

I, usually so vulnerable, could at last contemplate the struggle for life with considerable chance of success. My metamorphosis seemed to have completely come off, down to its innermost depths, and was approaching the level of a masterpiece, when I clearly heard two verses of Mallarmé in my hard, horned skull. Obviously the whole thing had to be started again.

—SUPERVIELLE

PARIS

Paris est l'endroit du monde où il est le plus facile de se passer de bonheur.
~ Paris is the place on earth where it is easiest to do without happiness.

—KAZIMIERZ BRANDYS

PEDAGOGY

~ Rocks and trees will teach you things that you cannot learn from any masters.

—SAINT BERNARD

~ Nothing that is worth knowing can be taught.

—OSCAR WILDE

~ All professors are not fools, but all fools are professors.

—NICOLÁS GÓMEZ DÁVILA

~ The intelligent man loves to learn, the fool loves to teach.

—CHEKHOV

~ Theory is the cold and lying tombstone of a departed truth.

—CONRAD

On n'explique que les choses mortes, et on finit par les tuer pour pouvoir les expliquer.
~ We can explain only dead things, and in the end we kill them in order to be able to explain them.

—MARIE-ALAIN COUTURIER

PHILOSOPHY

松風吹解帶。山月照彈琴。
君問窮通理。漁歌入浦深。

王維

~ The breeze in the pine-trees makes my belt flutter. In the mountain, I play the zither under the moon. You ask me what is the last word of philosophy? It is the song of a fisherman returning to shore.

—WANG WEI

~ There are nowadays professors of philosophy, but not philosophy. To be a philosopher is not merely to have subtle thoughts, nor even to found a school, but so to love wisdom as to live according to its dictates, a life of simplicity, independence, magnanimity and trust. It is to solve some of the problems of life, not only theoretically, but practically.

—THOREAU

Si tu attends de la philosophie qu'elle t'apprenne des choses, eh bien, tu peux être tranquille, elle ne t'apprendra rien du tout. Mais si tu te contentes d'y voir une invitation à te faire toi-même *ta philosophie, il te reste un peu d'espoir. Remarque que tous les bons philosophes ont tous été des antiphilosophes: Schopenhauer, Nietzsche, Locke et les autres. Ils ont tous été un peu ce que le* Canard enchaîné *est au* Figaro *[…] Apprends un peu, et tu deviendras toi-même un philosophe, ce qui est bien mieux que d'être un professeur de philosophie, ce qui est en tout cas beaucoup plus gai.*

~ If you expect philosophy to teach you things, you will be disappointed: it will teach you nothing. Yet, if you merely take it as an invitation to elaborate *your own* philosophy, you may get something out of it. Note that all the good philosophers were anti-philosophers: Schopenhauer, Nietzsche, Locke and others. To some extent, they were what *Punch* is to *The Times* [...] Learn a little, and you will become a philosopher yourself, which is much better than a professor of philosophy, or at least much more fun.

—J. PAULHAN*

~ What is the use of studying philosophy if all it does for you is to enable you to talk with some plausibility about some abstruse questions of logic, etc., and if it does not improve your thinking about the important questions of everyday life [...] You see, I know that it's difficult to think *well* about 'certainty', 'probability', 'perception', etc. But it is, if possible, still more difficult to think, or *try* to think, really honestly about your life and other people's lives. And the trouble is that thinking about these things is *not thrilling*, but often downright nasty. And when it's nasty, then it's most important.

—WITTGENSTEIN

POET

~ In every man there is the soul of a poet, but most of them are such bad ones.

—COLERIDGE

---

* Letter to his son.

~ Just like a bad man is nevertheless a man, so a bad poet is nevertheless a poet.

—CHESTERTON

~ To think clearly in human terms you have to be impelled by a poem.

—LES MURRAY

POLEMICIST

Un polémiste est amusant jusqu'à la vingtième année, tolérable jusqu'à la trentième, assommant vers la cinquantaine, et obscène au-delà.
~ A polemicist is amusing till age twenty, tolerable till thirty, boring around fifty, and beyond that, obscene.

—BERNANOS

POLITICS

~ The desire to go into politics is usually indicative of some sort of personality disorder, and it is precisely those who want power most that should be kept furthest from it.

—ARTHUR KOESTLER

~ Great writers and artists should take part in politics only as a defence against politics.

—CHEKHOV

~ There is always a certain meanness in the arguments of the conservatives, combined with a certain superiority in their facts.

—EMERSON

Une société bien faite serait celle où l'État n'aurait qu'une action négative de l'ordre du gouvernail: une légère pression au moment opportun pour compenser un commencement de déséquilibre.
~ A well-run society is a society where the State needs to act only in a negative way, like the rudder of a boat: a light pressure at the right time to counter an incipient imbalance.

—SIMONE WEIL

治大國若烹小鮮

老子

~ Govern a big country as you would cook a small fish.

—LAO ZI

Le social est irréductiblement le domaine du Prince de ce monde. On n'a d'autre devoir à l'égard du social que de tenter de limiter le mal.

~ Society is irreducibly the domain of the Devil. Our only duty to society is to try to contain the evil.

—SIMONE WEIL

POVERTY

~ The prevalent fear of poverty among our educated classes is the worst moral disease from which our civilisation suffers.

—WILLIAM JAMES

~ There is nothing in the world more favourable to genius than leisurely poverty.

—UNAMUNO

~ None can be an impartial or wise observer of human life, but from the vantage ground of what we should call voluntary poverty.

—THOREAU

POWER

~ Give a man power over other men, and he deteriorates at once.

—E. M. FORSTER

~ The mass of the people never get the chance to bring their innate decency into the control of affairs, so that one is almost driven to the cynical thought that men are only decent when they are powerless.

— ORWELL

PRAYER

Rappelant à Jésus notre dénuement extrême, je lui disais: 'Donnez-moi ce qu'il y a dans votre main, ouvrez votre main.' Alors il a ouvert sa main, et j'ai vu qu'elle était percée!

La seule vraie dévotion, c'est la pitié pour Jésus, c'est-à-dire la compassion de Marie. Il faut prier. Tout le reste est vain et stupide. Il faut prier pour endurer l'horreur de ce monde. Il n'y a ni désespoir ni tristesse amère pour l'homme qui prie beaucoup. C'est moi qui vous le dis. Si vous saviez combien j'en ai le droit et avec quelle autorité je vous parle! Il s'agit de prier simplement, bêtement, mais avec un vouloir puissant. Il est indispensable de prier longtemps, patiemment, sans écouter le dégoût, ni la fatigue, jusqu'à ce que l'émotion vienne et qu'on sente comme un tison dans le cœur. Alors on peut aller en paix et subir n'importe quoi.

~ Reminding Jesus of our extreme destitution, I told him: 'Give me what is in your hand, open your hand.' He then opened his hand, and *I saw that it was pierced.*

89

The only true devotion is pity for Jesus, which is to say the compassion of Mary. One must pray. Everything else is useless and stupid. For he who prays much, there can be no despair nor bitter grief. I am telling this to you, and I have the right to do so, and I speak with true authority! You must pray simply, naïvely, yet with a powerful will. The main thing is to pray for a long time, patiently, without yielding to disgust nor to fatigue, until emotion arises and you feel as if you had a firebrand in your heart. Then you may go in peace and face any tribulation.

—LÉON BLOY

PREJUDICE

~ [Recipe for avoiding condescension in racial relations] My question is usually: would this person be endurable if white?

—FLANNERY O'CONNOR

Il faut bien connaître les préjugés de son siècle, afin de ne les choquer pas trop, ni trop les suivre.
~ One must be well aware of the prejudices of one's time, in order not to offend them blindly nor to follow them blindly.

—MONTESQUIEU

PRIEST

*Si j'avais été chrétien croyant, j'aurais été prêtre. Et
j'aurais été un saint. Car un croyant est un saint, ou il
n'est pas croyant. Le sacerdoce fait de tout homme qui l'a
reçu un séparé. S'il n'est plus un séparé, il n'est rien.*

*Le pauvre prêtre. – Je le rencontre souvent, dans un
certain quartier. Le seul de Paris à porter soutane, n'en
doutons pas. Toujours tête nue, cheveux blancs, et le
visage d'un centenaire. La soutane propre, mais des
godillots de clochard. Une fois, je l'ai vu faisant la queue,
sur le trottoir, devant une marchande de comestibles. Si
j'avais été la marchande, je lui aurais dit: 'Monsieur
l'Abbé, passez le premier.'*

Il est d'un autre monde. Il est du sien.

*J'aurais voulu trouver l'occasion – circonstances, lieu,
ambiance – de me mettre à genoux devant lui et de lui
demander sa bénédiction.*

~ Had I been a Christian believer, I would have been
a priest. And I would have been a saint. For a believer
must be a saint, otherwise he is not a believer. Priest-
hood turns the man vested with it into a separate person. If he ceases to be separate, he is nothing.

The poor priest. – I often come across him in a certain suburb. He must be the only one in Paris still wear-
ing a cassock. Always bare-headed, with white hair and

the face of a man who is a hundred years old. His cassock is clean but he wears the boots of a tramp. Once, I saw him waiting in a queue on the pavement at the door of a grocery shop. Had I been the grocer, I would have told him, 'Monsieur l'abbé, come in first.'

He belongs to another world. His own.

I would have wished to find a chance – right circumstances, place and time – to kneel in front of him and ask for his blessing.

—Montherlant

Tout prêtre qui ne tend pas à la sainteté est réellement, rigoureusement, absolument un Judas et une ordure.

Le curé de B… nous intéresse. Il a vraiment l'air de croire en Dieu.

~ Every priest who does not aspire to sainthood is really, strictly and absolutely a Judas and a scum.

The parish priest of B… is an interesting case. He actually seems to believe in God.

—Léon Bloy

PROUST

Le passé quand l'imagination ne s'y complaît pas, au moment où quelque rencontre le fait surgir dans sa pureté, est du temps à couleur d'éternité. Le sentiment

de la réalité y est pur. C'est là la joie pure. C'est là le
beau. Proust.

~ The past, when imagination is not playing with
it, just at the instant when a chance encounter brings
it back in its purity, is time in the colour of eternity. It
affords a feeling of pure reality. This is pure joy. This is
beauty. Proust.

—SIMONE WEIL

~ Really the things we remember are the things we
forget. When a memory comes back sharply and suddenly, piercing the protection of oblivion, it appears for
an instant exactly as it really was. If we think of it often,
while its essentials remain true, it becomes more and
more our own memory of the thing rather than the
thing remembered.

—CHESTERTON

PROVIDENCE

Tout ce qui arrive est adorable, je le maintiens avec toute
l'autorité de ma misère qui est parfaite comme Dieu est
parfait, et qui est adorable par conséquent.

~ Whatever happens is adorable. I maintain this with
the full authority of my own misery, which is perfect as
God himself is perfect, and therefore also adorable.

—LÉON BLOY

RAIN

少年聽雨歌樓上。紅燭昏羅帳。
壯年聽雨客舟中。江闊雲低。斷雁
叫西風。而今聽雨僧廬下。鬢已
星星也。悲欢離合總無情。一任
階前点滴到天明。

　　　　　蒋捷

~ In my youth, I used to listen to the rain in the houses of sing-song girls; the lights of red candles were dancing on silk curtains.

In middle age, I have listened to the rain as I travelled on board boats on the broad river; under low clouds, a wild goose that had lost its mates was calling in the west wind.

But tonight I am listening to the rain in a hermit's hut; my hair has turned white; all passion spent – grief and joy, separation and reunion – I let the drops drip on the front steps till daybreak.

—Jiang Jie

READING

~ We read in order to know that we are not alone.

—C. S. LEWIS

~ A man ought to read just as inclination leads him; for what he reads as a task will do him little good.

—SAMUEL JOHNSON

Au fond, la plupart des gens ne lisent pas; ou, s'ils lisent, ils ne comprennent pas; quant à ceux qui comprennent, ils oublient.

~ After all, most people do not read; those who read don't understand; and those who do understand forget.

—MONTHERLANT

~ It makes no difference what I read. If it is irrelevant, I read it deeper. I read it until it is pertinent to me, and mine. There is creative reading as well as creative writing.

—EMERSON

J'ai pris la résolution de ne lire que de bons livres; celui qui lit les mauvais est semblable à un homme qui passe sa vie en mauvaise compagnie.

~ I resolved to read only good books. He who reads bad ones is like a man who spends his time in bad company.

—MONTESQUIEU

~ The art of *not* reading is a very important one. It consists of not taking an interest in whatever may be engaging the attention of the general public at any particular time. When some political or ecclesiastical pamphlet or novel or poem is making a great commotion, you should remember that he who writes for fools always finds a large public. A precondition for reading good books is not reading bad ones: for life is short.

—SCHOPENHAUER

~ Reading long at one time anything, no matter how it fascinates, destroys thought. Do not permit this. Stop if you find yourself becoming absorbed, at even the first paragraph.

—EMERSON

~ Only he who takes what he writes directly out of his own head is worth reading.

—SCHOPENHAUER

~ I forget most of what I have read, just as I do most of what I have eaten, but I know that both contribute no less to the conservation of my mind and my body on that account.

—LICHTENBERG

~ The difference between the effect produced on the mind by thinking for yourself and that produced by reading is incredibly great […] Much reading robs the mind of all elasticity, as the continual pressure of a weight does a spring, and the surest way of never having any thought of your own is to pick up a book every time you have a free moment. The practice of doing this is the reason erudition makes most men duller and sillier than they are by nature and robs their writing of all effectiveness.

—SCHOPENHAUER

~ We begin reading early and we often read too much, so that we receive and retain large amounts of material without putting it into employment, and our memory becomes accustomed to keeping open house for taste and feeling; this being so, we often have need of a profound philosophy to restore to our feelings their original state of innocence, to find *our* way out of the rubble of things alien to us, to begin to feel for *ourselves* and to speak *ourselves*, and I might almost say, to exist ourselves.

—Lichtenberg

Il ne faut pas beaucoup de livres quand on sait lire [...] Apprenez à méditer sur quelques lignes d'un auteur même médiocre; rien ne sert que ce qui a été fondé par la méditation.

~ If you know how to read, you do not need many books [...] Learn to meditate on a few lines, even from a mediocre author; nothing bears fruit unless it is rooted in meditation.

—Lacordaire

~ To read is to translate, for no two persons' experiences are the same. A bad reader is like a bad translator: he interprets literally when he ought to paraphrase, and paraphrases when he ought to interpret literally. In learning to read well, scholarship, valuable as it is, is less important than instinct; some great scholars have been poor translators.

—W. H. Auden

REALITY

桃花流水杳然去
別有天地非人間
　　　　李白

~ Peach blossoms are carried far away by flowing
waters into a world that is not the world of men.

—Li Bai

*On croit à la réalité de trop de choses. Ce journal en est
pour moi une preuve. Je consigne ici les moindres faits
avec un soin méticuleux. Lorsqu'un peu de temps s'est
écoulé, je m'étonne d'avoir donné tant d'importance à ce
qui en avait si peu. Les événements ou incidents qui
avaient agi sur mon âme s'aplanissent, s'effacent à une
certaine distance, ont l'air de rentrer dans le néant d'où
ils ne sont probablement jamais sortis. Il ne reste que ce
que l'on a fait ou souffert pour Dieu.*

*Tout n'est qu'apparence, tout n'est que symbole, même
la douleur la plus déchirante. Nous sommes des dor-
mants qui crient dans leur sommeil. Nous ne pouvons
jamais savoir si telle chose qui nous afflige n'est pas le
principe secret de notre joie ultérieure.*

~ We believe in the reality of too many things. My diary provides evidence of this. I am noting here the smallest incidents with meticulous care. After a little while I am amazed by the importance I had given to things that did not have any. Events or incidents that had affected my soul become insignificant and disappear, fade into the distance, they revert to a nothingness which they probably never left. The only things that remain are those which we did or suffered for God.

Everything is mere appearance, everything is mere symbol, even the most excruciating pain. We are all sunk in a deep slumber and are crying in our sleep. We can never know if those things that affect us now are not the secret principle of our future joy.

—Léon Bloy

~ The true meaning of spiritual is real.

—Emerson

RETIREMENT

~ Retirement – *Jubilación*.

—English–Spanish Dictionary

功成身退天之道
老子

~ To retire once the task is accomplished, this is the
Way of Heaven.

—LAO ZI

RITUAL

*Il ne faut sous-estimer ni les rites ni leur durée. Une
société ne peut se maintenir si elle n'est pas attachée
inconditionnellement à des valeurs, lesquelles, pour être
inconditionnelles, doivent avoir un aspect sensible qui
les protège du travail de sape de la raison.*

~ One should not underestimate rites and their dura-
tion. A society cannot maintain itself if it is not uncon-
ditionally attached to values which, in order to be
unconditional, must take some tangible form that pro-
tects them from being undermined by reason.

—CLAUDE LÉVI-STRAUSS

SACRED

~ The value of a profane thing lies in what it usefully
does, the value of a sacred thing lies in what it is.

—W. H. AUDEN

SAINT

Vivre sans vivre en saint, c'est vivre en insensé.
~ Not to lead a saint's life is to lead an insane life.

—Rancé

~ Holiness rather than peace.

—John Henry Newman

Il n'y a qu'une tristesse, et c'est de n'être pas des saints.
~ There is only one sorrow: not to be a saint.

—Léon Bloy

SANTAYANA

~ Everything that lives is tragic in its fate, comic in its existence, and lyric in its ideal existence.

—Santayana

SAVAGES

~ Don't cant in defence of savages.

—Samuel Johnson

SCHOLAR

Je n'aime pas les savants à moins qu'ils ne le soient sans le vouloir et sans le savoir. Il n'y a rien de si aisé que de le devenir. Qu'on s'enferme chez soi pendant six mois pour savoir, et l'on saura. Il vaut bien mieux avoir de l'imagination que de la mémoire. Qu'est-ce que c'est que tous ces dictionnaires ambulants? Les savants ne savent que des mots. Je ne vois jamais de savants de choses; c'est que ceux-ci n'ont pas la réputation de l'être. Les autres sont toujours orgueilleux, pédants, et à charge à une société. Le meilleur livre est le monde.

~ I do not like scholars, unless their learning is natural and without self-consciousness. Learning is easy to acquire. Lock yourself at home for six months and you will know whatever it is you set yourself to know. Imagination is much more valuable than memory. What use are all those walking dictionaries? Scholars only know words; I wish they knew things instead – the problem is that those who know things are not called scholars. Scholars are vain, pedantic and live as parasites on society. The best book is the world itelf.

—Prince de Ligne

~ People often become scholars for the same reason they become soldiers: simply because they are unfit for any other station.

—Lichtenberg

Quand on a fréquenté des érudits, il est facile de se ren-
dre compte qu'il n'y a pas de gens moins sûrs et qui se
rapprochent davantage du type du maniaque et de
l'aliéné. La science nous invitant constamment à de vas-
tes conclusions tirées de faibles données est un irritant,
un excitant vraiment dangereux pour l'imagination.
~ When one has had to deal with erudite academics,
one quickly realises that few minds are less sound or
closer to mania and insanity. As scholarly research
constantly invites us to draw large conclusions from
tenuous information, it inflames the imagination and
stimulates it dangerously.

—PAUL CLAUDEL

Cette pétrification de l'esprit propre au mandarin – tout
savant est un peu cadavre.
~ Petrification of the mind is typical of the mandarin
– every scholar is partly a cadaver.

—VICTOR HUGO

SEA

θάλασσα κλύζει πάντα τάνθρωπων κακά
~ The sea washes away all the evils of men.

—EURIPIDES

Suave mari magno turbantibus aequora ventis
E terra magnum spectare alterius laborem.
~ When the storm is battering the waves, it is sweet to
watch from dry land the formidable struggle of those
who are at sea.

—LUCRETIUS

長恨此身非我有。何時忘却營營。
小舟從此逝。江海寄餘生。
蘇軾

~ I hate not to be the master of my own life! When at
last shall I be able to forsake the worries of this world
and, dropping the mooring of my little boat, entrust
my remaining years to the rivers and the sea?

—SU DONGPO

~ And suddenly I rejoiced in the great security of the
sea as compared with the unrest of the land, in my
choice of that untempted life presenting no disquieting
problems, invested with an elementary moral beauty
by the absolute straightforwardness of its appeal and by
the singleness of its purpose.

—CONRAD

~ It is not that life ashore is distasteful to me. But life at sea is better.

—Sir Francis Drake

Ces beaux et grands navires imperceptiblement balancés sur les eaux tranquilles, ces robustes navires à l'air désœuvré et nostalgique, ne nous disent-ils pas dans une langue muette et magique: Quand partons-nous pour le bonheur?
~ These beautiful tall ships gently rocking at anchor, these strong vessels that look idle and nostalgic – aren't they all telling us in their silent, magic language: When shall we set sail towards happiness?

—Baudelaire

~ The monotony of the sea is easier to bear than the boredom of the shore, if only because there is no visible remedy and no contrasts at hand to keep discontent alive. The world contains, or contained then, some people who could put up with a sense of peace for three months.

—Conrad

Qu'il y ait toujours à notre porte cette aube immense appelée mer.

~ Let there always be on our doorstep this immense dawn we call the sea.

—Saint-John Perse

~ Haven't we, together and upon the immortal sea, wrung out a meaning from our sinful lives?

—Conrad

La vie de la plupart des hommes est un chemin mort et ne mène à rien. Mais d'autres savent, dès l'enfance, qu'ils vont vers une mer inconnue. Déjà l'amertume du vent les étonne, déjà le goût du sel est sur leurs lèvres – jusqu'à ce que, la dernière dune franchie, cette passion infinite les soufflette de sable et d'écume. Il leur reste de s'y abîmer ou de revenir sur leurs pas.

~ Most people's lives follow an arid path that leads nowhere. But others know, from childhood, that they are heading towards an unknown sea. Already they feel a strange wildness in the wind that brings a taste of salt to their lips – and then suddenly, having climbed a last sand dune, they find themselves facing this infinite passion which buffets them with its myriad stings of sand and spray. Now is the time to choose: either to throw themselves forward – or to turn back.

—F. Mauriac

La mer, cette patrie qui voyage avec nous …
~ The sea, this motherland which travels with us …
—CHATEAUBRIAND

~ And yet the sea is a horrible place, stupefying to the mind and poisonous to the temper; the sea, the motion, the lack of space, the cruel publicity, the villainous tinned foods, the sailors, the captain, the passengers – but you are amply repaid when you sight an island, and drop anchor in a new world.
—R. L. STEVENSON

Iucundissima navigatio juxta terram, ambulatio juxta mare.
~ The most pleasant navigation is along the shore, the most pleasant walk is along the sea.
—ERASMUS*

~ By all that's wonderful, it is the sea, I believe, the sea itself – or is it youth alone? Who can tell? But you here – you all had something out of life: money, love – whatever one gets on shore – and tell me, wasn't that the best time, that time when we were young at sea; young and had nothing, on the sea that gives nothing, except

* Erasmus was really a landlubber. For sailors, coastal navigation is the most uncomfortable.

hard knocks – and sometimes a chance to feel your
strength – that only – what you all regret?

—CONRAD

~ The people along the sand
  All turn and look one way
  They turn their back on the land
  They look at the sea all day

      *   *   *

  They cannot look out far
  They cannot look in deep
  But when was that ever a bar
  To any watch they keep?

—ROBERT FROST

SERIOUSNESS

La gravité est le plaisir des sots.
~ Seriousness is the pleasure of fools.

—A. VIALATTE

*Un homme sérieux a peu d'idées. Un homme à idées
n'est jamais sérieux.*
~ A serious man has few ideas. A man with ideas is
never serious.

—PAUL VALÉRY

SEX

子曰。吾未見好德如好色者也。

論語

~ The Master said: I have never seen anyone who loved virtue as much as sex.

—ANALECTS OF CONFUCIUS

~ Love between man and man is impossible because there must not be sexual intercourse, and friendship between man and woman is impossible because there must be sexual intercourse.

—JAMES JOYCE

SHIT

Stercus cuique bene olet.
~ Everyone finds his own shit smells good.

—ERASMUS

Cuando merda tiver valor, pobre nasce sem cu.
~ If shit were valuable, the poor would be born without arses.

—PORTUGUESE PROVERB

SILENCE

子曰。予欲無言。子貢曰。子如不言。則小子
何述焉。子曰。天何言哉。四時行焉。百物
生焉。天何言哉。

論語

~ The Master said: 'I wish to speak no more.' Zigong said: 'Master, if you do not speak, how would little ones like us still be able to hand down any teachings?' The Master said: 'Does Heaven speak? Yet the four seasons follow their course and the hundred creatures continue to be born. Does Heaven speak?'

—ANALECTS OF CONFUCIUS

Aut tace aut loquere meliora silentio.
~ Keep silent unless what you say is better than silence.

—SALVATOR ROSA

言而當知也。默而當亦知也。

荀子

~ To speak to the point is wisdom; to be silent to the point is also wisdom.

—XUN ZI

SIMPLICITY

~ Great simplicity [of literary expression] is only won by an intense moment, or by years of intelligent effort, or by both. It represents one of the most arduous conquests of the human spirit: the triumph of feeling and thought over the natural sin of language.

—T. S. ELIOT

SMALLNESS

~ We fought so much against small things that we have ourselves become small.

—EUGENE O'NEILL

SOCIETY

Nolite conformari huic saeculo.
~ Do not follow the fashions of the world.

—SAINT PAUL

Le social est irréductiblement le domaine du diable.
~ Society is irreducibly the domain of the Devil.

—SIMONE WEIL

~ I only know that he who forms a tie is lost. The germ of corruption has entered his soul.

—CONRAD

廉頗失勢之時。故客盡去。及復用為將
客又復至。廉頗曰。客退矣。客曰。吁。君何
見之晚也。夫天下以市道交。君有勢。
我則從君。君無勢則去。此固其理也。
何怨乎。

史記

~ When Lian Po lost his office, all his retainers left
him. After he was restored to it, his retainers wanted to
come back to him. Lian Po told them: 'Go away!' One
of them replied: 'How naïve can you be? Don't you
know that social relations are ruled by the laws of the
marketplace? When you occupy an influential position, we follow you. If you lose it, we go. All this is quite
sensible. Why fret?'

—SIMA QIAM

La rareté d'un sentiment vrai *fait que je m'arrête quelquefois dans les rues à regarder un chien ronger un os.
'C'est au retour de Versailles (disait M. de …) que je suis
plus curieux de ce spectacle.'*
~ The rarity of a *true* feeling sometimes makes me
stop in the street to watch a dog gnawing a bone. 'It is
on my way back from the Royal Court (Mr de B…
said) that I am most keen to watch such a spectacle.'

—CHAMFORT

113

La confusion mentale est pathologique quand on est seul, normale quand on est plusieurs.
~ Mental confusion is pathological when one is alone, normal when in a group.

—Paul Valéry

SOLITUDE

O beata solitudo, o sola beatitudo!
~ O blessed solitude, o sole blessing!

—Saint Bernard

Qui me rend visite me fait honneur, qui ne me rend pas visite me fait plaisir.
~ He who pays me a visit honours me; he who does not pay me a visit gives me pleasure.

—Montherlant

Solitude. En quoi donc en consiste le prix? Le prix en consiste dans la possibilité supérieure d'attention.
~ Solitude. What makes it so precious? Its value lies in an increased possibility for attention.

—Simone Weil

Il faut avoir femme, enfants, biens et surtout de la santé, qui peut; mais non pas s'y attacher en manière que notre heur en dépende. Il se faut réserver une arrière-boutique toute nôtre, toute franche, en laquelle nous établissons notre vraie liberté et principale retraite et solitude. En celle-ci faut-il prendre notre ordinaire entretien de nous-mêmes, et si privé que nulle accointance ou communication étrangère y trouve place; discourir et y rire comme sans femme, sans enfants et sans biens, sans train et sans valets, afin que, quand l'occasion adviendra de leur perte, il ne nous soit pas nouveau de nous en passer. Nous avons une âme contournable en soi-même; elle se peut faire compagnie; elle a de quoi assaillir et de quoi défendre, de quoi recevoir et de quoi donner; ne craignons pas en cette solitude nous croupir d'oisiveté ennuyeuse.

~ We should have wives, children, property, and above all good health if we can; but we should not become so attached to them that our happiness depends on them. We should set aside a room, just for ourselves, in the back of the shop, keeping it entirely free and establishing there our true liberty, our principal solitude and asylum. Within it our normal conversation should be with ourselves, so private that no commerce or communication with the outside world should find a place there; there we should talk and laugh as though we had no wife, no children, no possessions, no followers, no manservants, so that when the occasion arises that we must lose them it should not be a new experience to do without them. We have a soul able to turn in on herself, she can keep herself company, she has the wherewithal to attack, to defend, to receive and to give. Let us not fear that in such a solitude as that we would rot away in morose idleness.*

—MONTAIGNE

~ When a man has reached old age and has fulfilled his mission, he has a right to confront the idea of death in peace. He has no need of other men, he knows them already and he has seen enough of them. What he needs is peace. It is not seemly to seek out such a man, plague him with chatter and make him suffer banalities. One should pass by the door of his house as if no one lived there.

—H. HESSE

Je n'ai jamais vécu avec les gens du monde, et je crois difficilement à ceux qui habitent dans cette mer où le flot pousse le flot sans que jamais rien n'y prenne consistance. Je crois la solitude aussi nécessaire à l'amitié qu'à la sainteté, au génie qu'à la vertu.

~ I have never lived in worldly society and would have difficulty trusting those who inhabit that sea where one

---

* M. A. Screech translation, slightly modified (Penguin Classics).

wave pushes the other and nothing ever acquires consistency. I believe solitude to be equally necessary for friendship and for holiness, for genius and for virtue.

—Lacordaire

STRAIGHTFORWARDNESS

~ [The Galapogos tortoises never go round any obstacle; they remain stuck against it, be it a rock or a main-mast.] They hold on their inflexible path. Their crowning curse is their drudging impulse to straightforwardness in a belittered world.

—Melville

SWORD

~ Those who take the sword perish by the sword, and those who don't take the sword perish by smelly diseases.

—Orwell

TALENT

Tout le monde a du talent à vingt-cinq ans. La difficulté est d'en avoir à cinquante.
~ Everyone has talent at twenty-five. The difficulty is to have it at fifty.

—Degas

TASTE

~ The moment good taste knows itself some of its goodness is lost.

—C. S. LEWIS

Le mauvais goût mène au crime.
~ Bad taste leads to crime.

—STENDHAL

~ Nothing makes one feel so unclean as simulating enthusiasm.

—J. POPE-HENNESSY

TIME

Dans la douleur ou dans la joie, nous croyons que le temps est quelque chose, et il n'est rien, puisqu'il n'existe pas pour Dieu, il ne devrait donc pas exister pour nous. C'est lui qui nous sépare de Dieu. Si nous obtenions cette grâce de ne jamais savoir l'heure, nous serions déjà dans l'Éternité bienheureuse et la souffrance, alors, serait pour nous comme une barque rapide sur un affluent du Paradis.

~ In pain or in joy, we believe that time is something real, whereas it is nothing; since it does not exist for God, it should not exist for us. Time separates us from

God. If we could be blessed never to know what time it is, we would already have reached blissful Eternity, and then every suffering would be for us like a swift little boat on a stream flowing into Paradise.

—LÉON BLOY

~ For we are so little reconciled to time that we are even astonished by it. 'How he's grown!' we exclaim, 'How time flies', as though the universal form of our experience were again and again a novelty. It is as strange as if a fish were repeatedly surprised at the wetness of water. And that would be strange indeed, unless, of course, the fish were destined to become, one day, a land animal. We have a strange illusion that mere time cancels sin. But mere time does nothing either to the fact or to the guilt of a sin. The guilt is washed out not by time but by repentance and the blood of Christ.

—C. S. LEWIS

TOAD

M. de Lassay, homme très doux, mais qui avait une grande connaissance de la société, disait qu'il faudrait avaler un crapaud tous les matins, pour ne trouver plus rien de dégoûtant le reste de la journée quand on devait la passer dans le monde.

~ Mr de Lassay, a very sweet gentleman with a great knowledge of the ways of the world, used to say that one should swallow a toad every morning, so as to find nothing disgusting for the rest of the day when one has to spend it in society.

—Chamfort

Donner sa somme dans son produit, c'est le triomphe de quiconque crée. La crapaude qui fait un crapaud fait un chef-d'œuvre. Vous doutez? Essayez d'en faire autant.
~ To put all of oneself into one's creation is a triumph. The female toad who produces another toad achieves a masterpiece. You doubt it? Just try to do the same.

—Victor Hugo

TOBACCO

~ Insanity has grown more frequent since smoking has gone out of fashion.

—Samuel Johnson

TRANSLATION

Je m'apercevais que, pour exprimer ces impressions, pour écrire ce livre essentiel, le seul livre vrai, un grand écrivain n'a pas, dans le sens courant, à l'inventer, puisqu'il existe déjà en chacun de nous, mais à le traduire. Le devoir et la tâche d'un écrivain sont ceux d'un traducteur.

~ I came to realise that, in order to express these impressions, in order to write this essential book, the only true book, a great writer does not have to invent it in the ordinary sense of the word, since it already exists in every one of us – he must translate it. The duty and the task of a writer are those of a translator.

—PROUST

La vraie manière d'écrire est d'écrire comme on traduit. Quand on traduit un texte écrit dans une langue étrangère, on ne cherche pas à y ajouter, on met au contraire un scrupule religieux à ne rien ajouter. C'est ainsi qu'il faut essayer de traduire un texte non écrit.
~ The only way to write is to write as if we were translating. When we translate a text written in a foreign language, we do not add anything to it; on the contrary, we endeavour scrupulously to add nothing to it. That's how one must attempt to translate an unwritten text.

—SIMONE WEIL

TRAVEL

Caelum non animum mutant qui trans mare currunt.
~ Those who cross the seas find themselves under other skies with the same minds.

—HORACE

Voyager est, quoi qu'on en puisse dire, un des plus tristes plaisirs de la vie. Lorsque vous vous trouvez bien dans une ville étrangère, c'est que vous commencez à vous y faire une patrie; mais traverser des pays inconnus, entendre parler un langage que vous comprenez à peine, voir des visages humains sans relation avec votre passé ni avec votre avenir, c'est de la solitude et de l'isolement sans repos et sans dignité; car cet empressement, cette hâte pour arriver là où personne ne vous attend, cette agitation dont la curiosité est la seule cause, vous inspire peu d'estime pour vous-même.

~ Whatever you may say, travel is one of the saddest pleasures of life. When you begin to feel comfortable in a foreign city, it is because it has progressively become another home for you; however, to cross strange lands, to hear languages you scarcely understand, to see human faces that bear no relation to your past or your future, all these are a form of loneliness and isolation devoid of peace and dignity; for this eagerness, this haste to arrive in some place where no one is waiting for you, this frantic activity whose sole motivation is curiosity, is conducive to very little self-respect.

—MADAME DE STAËL

*On part de Dieu pour aller à Dieu, et c'est le seul déplace-
ment qui ait un sens appréciable, une utilité. Tout le
reste, c'est-à-dire tout voyage où l'on croit aller quelque
part, est exactement stupide.*

~ We start from God and go to God. This is the only
meaningful move, the only useful one. All the rest, to
wit, any journey which you believe should take you
somewhere else, is simply stupid.

—Léon Bloy

Il y a tant de bel ascétisme dans tout départ.

~ There is such beautiful asceticism in every depar-
ture.

—Victor Segalen

TRIALS, SUFFERING

Forsan et haec olim meminisse iuvabit.

~ Perhaps, one day, you will even enjoy the memory
of all this.

—Virgil

*L'homme a des endroits de son pauvre cœur qui n'existent
pas encore, et où la douleur entre, afin qu'ils soient.*

~ There are places in man's wretched heart that do
not yet exist; suffering enters into them in order that
they may come into being.

—Léon Bloy

~ Pain comes from the darkness
And we call it wisdom.
It is pain.

—RANDALL JARRELL

Nous sommes tous des farceurs, nous survivons à nos problèmes.
~ We are all phonies: we survive our problems.

—CIORAN

TRUTH

Sic amatur veritas ut, quicumque aliud amant, hoc quod amant, velint esse veritatem, et quia falli nolent, nolunt convinci quod falsi sint.
~ Men's love for truth is such that, if they love something else, they wish it to be the truth; and since they do not want to be proved wrong, they refuse to accept that they were mistaken.

—SAINT AUGUSTINE

Tout ce que je conçois comme vrai est moins vrai que les choses dont je ne puis concevoir la vérité, mais que j'aime. Saint Jean de la Croix appelle la foi une nuit.

~ Whatever I may conceive as true is less true than the things whose truth I cannot conceive, but which I love. Saint John of the Cross calls faith a dark night.

—SIMONE WEIL

~ Truth is only believed when someone has invented it well.

—SANTAYANA

[En art] on donne l'idée du vrai avec du faux.
~ [In art] truth is suggested by false means.

—DEGAS

On ne peut jamais trop résister à Dieu, si on le fait par pur souci de vérité. Le Christ aime qu'on lui préfère la vérité car avant d'être le Christ, il est la vérité. Si on se détourne de lui pour aller vers la vérité, on ne fera pas un long chemin sans tomber dans ses bras.
~ One can never resist God too much if one resists him out of pure attachment to the truth. Christ welcomes those who follow the truth rather than him, since, before being Christ, he is the truth. If one turns away from him in order to pursue truth, one will not go very far without falling into his arms.

—SIMONE WEIL

UNIVERSAL FREEDOM

~ Earning a wage is a prison occupation
and a wage earner is a sort of gaol-bird.
Earning a salary is a prison overseer's job
a gaoler instead of a gaol-bird.
Living on your income is strolling grandly outside
the prison, in terror lest you have to go in. And since
the work prison covers
almost every scrap of the living earth, you stroll up
and down
on a narrow beat, about the same as a prisoner
taking his exercise.
This is called universal freedom.

—D. H. LAWRENCE

WEALTH

~ A man is rich in proportion to the number of things
which he can afford to let alone.

—THOREAU

WIFE

*Un bon critique aussi, c'est l'épouse; elle vous fait sentir
le peu que vous êtes.*
~ Another good critic: your wife – she helps you to
realise how small you are.

—JACQUES CHARDONNE

WINE

~ The sway of alcohol over mankind is unquestionably due to its power to stimulate the mystical faculties of human nature, usually crushed to earth by cold facts and dry criticism of the sober hours. Sobriety diminishes, discriminates, and says no; drunkenness expands, unites, and says yes. It is in fact the great exciter of the yes function in man.

—WILLIAM JAMES

~ It is a misfortune of Thoreau's that he has no appetite. He neither eats nor drinks. What can you have in common with a man who does not know the difference between ice-cream and cabbage, and has no experience of wine or ale?

—EMERSON

J'ai toujours remarqué que les gens faux sont sobres, et la grand réserve de la table annonce assez souvent des mœurs feintes et des âmes doubles.
~ I have always observed that devious people are abstemious, and that a strict self-restraint at the table often betrays false morality and a duplicitous soul.

—JEAN-JACQUES ROUSSEAU

~ The most dangerous things and the chief evils of the world are spiritual things. It is only because drink is very nearly a spiritual pleasure, that it is so highly dangerous. Drink is not an animal pleasure; it belongs to the intellectual and emotional world. If materialism were true, people would be as intemperate over ham sandwiches and pork pies as they are now over drink. It is because man has a soul that he drinks, and because animals have no souls that they do not drink.

—CHESTERTON

WITHOUT TRACE

善行無轍迹
　　老子

~ Perfect action leaves no trace.

—LAO ZI

Arriver par le travail à effacer les traces du travail.
~ Through work, manage to erase all traces of work.

—DEGAS

松下問童子,言師採藥去。
只在此山中,雲深不知処。
　　　賈島

~ Under a pine tree, I ask the young servant where the hermit is. 'My master went to collect medicinal herbs' he replies, 'he is somewhere in this mountain, but with such a mist, I do not know where.'

—JIA DAO

~ I love goldfish: they move around without making any tracks.

—ISAK DINESEN

今朝郡齋冷忽念山中客澗底束荊薪
歸來煮白石欲持一瓢酒遠慰風雨夕
落葉滿空山何處尋行跡

韋応物

~ This morning my office in the Prefecture was cold. I suddenly remembered my friend who lives in the mountain. He must be gathering firewood in some gully and then will cook his meal over white stones. I wished to bring him a bottle of wine to comfort him through the windy and rainy night. Fallen leaves cover the empty mountain. How could I find his track?

—WEI YINGWU

WOMAN

Moins portée que les hommes à courir après des buts illusoires, les femmes ont aussi sur eux l'avantage d'être étrangères à l'histoire, et le changement historique les modifie moins. (Sainte-Beuve a fait à propos de je ne sais plus quelle dame d'autrefois cette remarque étonnante que toute femme est notre contemporaine.) Et elles sont capables d'accomplir sans dégoût leur tâche journalière une vie durant.

~ Less inclined than men to pursue illusory goals, women also enjoy the advantage of being somewhat alien to history – historical transformations exert less impact on them. (Sainte-Beuve, discussing some famous lady of the past, made the stunning observation that every woman is our contemporary.) And they manage to perform their daily chores all their lives without disgust.

—GEORGES RODITI

~ If a woman does not believe in a *man*, she believes essentially in nothing. She becomes willy-nilly a devil.

—D. H. LAWRENCE

~ There is no female Mozart because there is no female Jack the Ripper.

—CAMILLE PAGLIA

~ The last thing a woman will consent to discover in a man whom she loves, or on whom she simply depends, is want of courage.

—Conrad

~ Women see better than men. Men see lazily if they do not expect to act. Women see quite without any wish to act.

—Emerson

~ A woman's guess is much more accurate than a man's certainty.

—Kipling

WORK

Le travail est encore ce que les gens ont inventé de mieux pour ne rien faire de leur vie.
~ Work is what people invented the better to do nothing with their lives.

—R. Vaneigem

Le travail est une infamie.
~ Work is an infamy.

—Montherlant

無為

~ No zeal.

—TAOIST MAXIM

~ It is only stupid people who work, because when not
working they do not know what to do with themselves.

—SOMERSET MAUGHAM

~ The things one is paid a salary for doing are never,
in my experience, *serious,* never seem in the long run
of any particular use to anyone.

—M. MUGGERIDGE

~ Leonardo da Vinci also executed in Milan for the
Dominicans of Santa Maria delle Grazie a marvellous
and beautiful painting of the Last Supper, but he left it
unfinished for a long time, and the Prior used to keep
pressing him in the most importunate way, because he
was puzzled by Leonardo's habit of sometimes spend-
ing half a day at a time contemplating what he had
done so far; if the Prior had had his way, Leonardo
would have toiled like one of the labourers hoeing in
the garden, and never put his brush down for a moment.
Not satisfied with this, the Prior then complained to
the Duke. The Duke sent for Leonardo and very tact-

fully questioned him about the painting. Leonardo, knowing that he was dealing with a prince of acute and discerning intelligence, was willing (as he never had been with the Prior) to explain his mind at length; and so he talked to the Duke for a long time about the art of painting. He explained that *men of genius sometimes accomplish most when they work the least*, for, he added, they are thinking out inventions, and forming in their minds the perfect ideas which they subsequently express and reproduce with their hands.

—VASARI

宋元君將畫圖。眾史皆至。受揖而立。
舐筆和墨。在外者半。有一史後至者。
儃儃然不趨。受揖不立。因之舍。公使
人視之。則解衣般礴臝。君曰。可矣。
是真畫者也。

莊子

~ Lord Yuan of Song wanted to have some pictures painted. The crowd of court clerks all gathered in his presence, paid their respects and took their places in line, licking their brushes, mixing their inks, so many of them that there were more outside the room than inside it. There was one clerk who arrived late, sauntering in without the slightest haste. Having paid his respects, he did not take his place in line, but withdrew to a backroom. The ruler sent someone to see what he was doing, and it was found that he had taken off his clothes and sat there, cross-legged, doing nothing. 'Excellent!' said the ruler, 'this is a true artist!'

—ZHUANG ZI

~ There are some who complain of a man for doing nothing, there are some, still more mysterious and amazing, who complain of having nothing to do. When actually presented with some beautiful blank hours or days, they will grumble at their blankness. When given the gift of loneliness, which is the gift of liberty, they will cast it away, they will destroy it deliberately with some dreadful game with cards, or a little ball […] I cannot repress a shudder when I see them throwing away their hard-won holidays by doing something. For my own part, I can never get enough Nothing-to-do.

—CHESTERTON

~ Never do yourself what you can pay another to do for you.

—SOMERSET MAUGHAM

~ When prostitutes call themselves 'sex-workers', work has become a prostitution.

—WALTER BENJAMIN

WORLD HARMONY

Que chacun reste chez soi!

Les Maoris au Groenland, les Basques en Ethiopie, les Peaux-Rouges en Nouvelle-Guinée, les Picards à Samoa, les Esquimaux à Bratislava, les Papous en Wallonie et les Celtes en Sibérie.

~ Let everyone stay home!

Maoris in Greenland, Basques in Ethiopia, Redskins in New Guinea, Picards in Samoa, Eskimos in Bratislava, Papuans in Luxembourg and Celts in Siberia.

—LOUIS SCUTENAIRE

WRITER

~ All writers are vain, selfish and lazy, and at the very bottom of their motives there lies a mystery. Writing a book is a horrible exhausting struggle, like a long bout of some painful illness. One would never undertake such a thing if one were not driven on by some demon whom one can neither resist nor understand. For all one knows, that demon is simply the same instinct that makes a baby squall for attention.

—ORWELL

Je vis comme un agneau pour pouvoir écrire comme un lion.
~ I live like a lamb so that I may write like a lion.

—FLAUBERT

~ We work in the dark, we do what we can, we give what we have; our doubt is our passion, our passion is our task – and the rest is the madness of art.

—HENRY JAMES

~ A writer is a man to whom writing comes harder than to anyone else.

—THOMAS MANN

~ Most writers understand no more about literature than birds do about ornithology.

—M. REICH-RANICKI

Écrire, quelle disgrâce.
~ To write – what a disgrace!

—CIORAN

Le talent se sert de tout ce qu'il se rappelle, le génie de tout ce qu'il a su oublier.
~ Talent makes use of all that it remembers; genius, all that it has managed to forget.

—P. REVERDY

N'invitez pas plusieurs hommes de letters à la fois: un bossu préférera toujours la compagnie d'un aveugle à celle d'un autre bossu.

~ Never invite several writers together: a hunchback always prefers the company of a blind man to that of another hunchback.

—PAUL CLAUDEL

~ I hate a writer who's all writer.

—BYRON

~ Humility is not a virtue propitious to the artist. It is often pride, emulation, avarice, malice – all the odious qualities – which drive a man to complete, elaborate, refine, destroy, renew, his work until he has made something that gratifies his pride and envy and greed. And in doing so, he enriches the world more than the generous and good, though he may lose his own soul in the process. This is the paradox of artistic achievement.

—EVELYN WAUGH

As-tu remarqué que les gens qui deviennent de nos jours grands écrivains, ce sont ceux qui n'ont pas particulièrement cherché à être écrivains et chez qui la littérature a été un hasard, une sorte d'accident – mais leur préoccu-

pation essentielle était ailleurs [...] Au contraire, ceux qui ont tenu à écrire des livres pour écrire des livres, ceux qui ont d'abord voulu être littérateurs, sont devenus précisément des 'littérateurs' (au mauvais sens du mot).

~ Have you noticed that nowadays those who become great writers are people who originally never specifically intended to be writers; for them, literature happened by chance, as a sort of accident: their main concern was elsewhere [...] Conversely, those who set their minds on writing books *in order to write books,* those who aspired first and foremost to be literary men, have become precisely that: 'literary men' (in the bad sense of the word).

—J. PAULHAN

J'ai acheté deux cents vaches, et gagné du même coup le droit de ne plus me dire 'homme de lettres' mais vacher, ce qui me paraît bien préférable. En tant qu'homme de lettres et homme du monde, j'étais lié par une foule de nécessités superflues; en tant que vacher, je pourrai écrire ce que je pense.

~ I bought two hundred cows and by the same token acquired the right to call myself no longer 'man of letters' but cattleman – which seems to me much to be preferred. As a man of letters and man of the world,

I was fettered by countless superfluous obligations; as a cattleman, I shall be able to write what I think.

—BERNANOS

YOUTH

Les sociétés payent très cher le fait d'avoir constitué la jeunesse comme une entité séparée. C'est le signe que les générations en place ne sont plus sûres de leurs valuers [...] Les sociétés se maintiennent parce qu'elles sont capables de transmettre d'une génération à l'autre leurs principes et leurs valeurs. À partir du moment où elles se sentent incapables de rien transmettre, ou ne savent plus quoi transmettre et se reposent sur les générations qui suivent, elles sont malades.

~ A society which treats its young as a separate entity is going to pay a dreadful price for this shortsighted indulgence: it is a sign that the established generation has lost faith in its own values and is abdicating its responsibility [...] A society will survive only if it is capable of transmitting its principles and values from one generation to the next. As soon as it feels unable to transmit anything, or when it does not know any more what should be transmitted, it ceases to be able to maintain itself.

—CLAUDE LÉVI-STRAUSS

ZHUANG ZI

予惡乎知說生之非惑邪。予惡乎知惡
死之非弱喪而不知歸者邪。

莊子

~ Who can tell if my attachment to life is not an illusion? Who can tell if my horror of death is not simply the reaction of a man who, having left his native place in childhood, forgot the way home?

—ZHUANG ZI

140

INDEX OF AUTHORS

INDEX OF SUBJECTS

146

ACKNOWLEDGEMENT

Denise O'Dea and Chris Feik's sensitive editing was of great assistance to me in the preparation of this book. I owe them much gratitude for their unfailing care and patience.

S.L.